TRACING
your
ANCESTORS

TRACING *your* ANCESTORS

MARILYN YURDAN

David & Charles

A catalogue record for this book is available from the
British Library.

ISBN 0-7153-0029-6

Printed in Great Britain by Billings & Son Ltd
for David & Charles
Brunel House   Newton Abbot   Devon

Contents

There were the Scots
Who kept the Sabbath
And everything else
They could lay their hands on.

Then there were the Welsh
Who prayed on their knees
And their neighbours.

Thirdly there were the Irish
Who never knew what they wanted
But were willing to fight for it anyway.

Lastly there were the English
Who considered themselves a self-made nation
Thus relieving the Almighty
Of a dreadful responsibility.

On a Scottish teatowel

1
Introduction

The selection of works on family history is gradually increasing as more and more people are becoming interested in the subject. These books deal with the methods of researching one's family history in varying degrees of depth and a visit to the local library or bookshop will yield enough information for the beginner to be able to familiarise him- or herself with the basic sources available, together with their relevance and whereabouts.

Having found out the whereabouts of the records on which his or her ancestors are likely to feature, however, the genuine family historian will quickly tire of merely copying out lists of names, parishes and dates, impressive though they may look made up into a pedigree.

True family-history research (as opposed to genealogy) is the study of one's forebears, not only in relation to the immediate family, but also in the wider context of their background. This would include their position in the community, with all the social, economic, moral and religious commitments which this would have entailed. By comparison, genealogy, in the strict sense of the word, restricts itself to the proving of the line of descent of a family or individual, the end product being a pedigree rather than a piece of social history.

This book, then, is an attempt to break away from the traditional method of writing a guide to family-history research which deals with sources available, usually in chronological order, with these sources and the information they contain forming the chapter headings. Instead, this book takes as its focal points the main phases and events in the human life-cycle, and explores both them and the information it is possible to extract concerning them, from the relevant sources.

The emphasis, therefore, is on the human aspect of one's ancestors' lives, rather than on what some would consider dry and dusty old documents. This, I hope, should help to turn the family members into real people, with hopes, fears, disappointments and triumphs similar to those which you, their descendant, experience today.

You can read the chapters of this book in any order depending on which period of your ancestor's life is currently of interest to you. This will save going through several chapters in order to extract the relevant details.

As life becomes ever more standardised by centralisation and red tape, those interested in an older way of life have become increasingly aware of the necessity of doing something positive in order to preserve what remains of it. Springing up all over the country, and, indeed, all over the world, are a variety of societies, clubs and collections, some very learned, others much less so, but together covering every aspect of history both ancient and recent. Only a few examples are those bodies devoted to old photographs and postcards, dialects and folk-songs, not to mention family and local-history groups; even those people who would not have previously thought of themselves as being historically minded can find a sense of achievement and of identity when establishing contact with the past in any of its many aspects.

One's personal involvement alters one's view of history. It is easy to flick through a history book and to spare a thought for Queen Anne, for example, with her dropsical legs and all those children who died before she did with no-one of her own blood to succeed her on the British throne. Causes of death are sometimes a source of hilarity because the deaths of those who died, say, 300 years ago no longer have the power to move us today. Anyone could be forgiven the odd smile when reading through the entries below from a London Bill of Mortality for the month of August 1665. These are just a few of many causes of death cited:

Disease or affliction	Number dying
'Frighted'	1
'Griping in the Guts'	74
'Imposthume' (abscess)	18
'King's Evil'	10
'Lethargy'	1
'Rising of the Lights'	19

Disease or affliction	Number dying
'Scouring' (prolonged diarrhoea)	13
'Sore Legge'	1
'Starved at Nurse'	1
'Stopping of the Stomach'	16
'Suddenly'	1
'Surfeit'	87
'Teeth'	113
'Winde'	8
'Wormes'	18

It is a little different, however, when you discover that your own great-great-great grandfather lay for days with a broken back after falling from a hayrick, and then died in agony surrounded by his family. Similarly, one realises how near one came to never being born at all when one reads of great-grandma being christened at home because everyone was convinced that she was going to die within the day (even if she did live to be eighty-nine just to prove them wrong!)

The number of ancestors that have played a part in producing one present-day individual gives much food for thought. Many of today's graduates and professional people, should they bother to trace their ancestry, might well be surprised to learn that they owe their brains or business acumen to farm labourers, servants or carpet-beaters, perhaps only three or four generations back. Conversely, those of us whose families have lived and worked in the countryside for generations may be equally surprised to find that we, like Tess of the D'Urbervilles, bear surnames which are corruptions of Norman ones, and that our ancestors did indeed 'come over with the Conqueror'.

At this point it should perhaps be mentioned that the Norman army of invasion included its fair share of manual workers, labourers, rough soldiery and just plain old-fashioned yobs, so that not everyone of Norman descent need feel themselves superior to those of plain Saxon stock.

While it is pleasant and proper enough to attempt a sentimental journey back through the centuries, with ancestors as escorts, it would be a pity to confine our attentions to the dead. In our eagerness to rush off and work our way back through documents and registers, it is only too

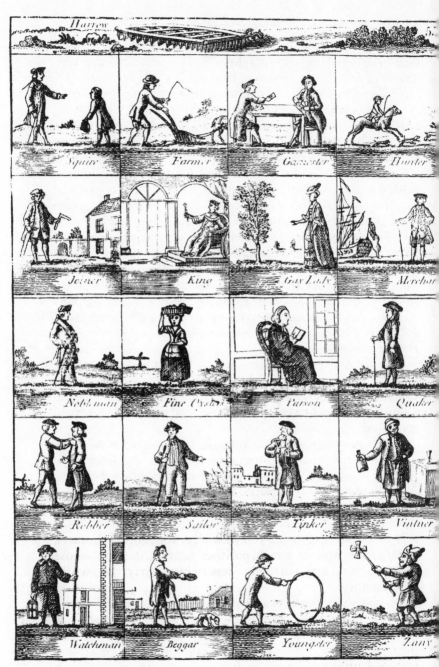

Conditions and occupations as illustrated in an eighteenth-century children's book

10

easy to forget our living relatives, particularly those whom we have never met. There might even be some whose very existence is as yet unknown to us.

The journals of family-history societies are a good way of making contact with others likely to share a common ancestry or researching the same name. It is also another means of getting someone to help with the work-load of contacting every known relative. Apart from the pleasure of making new friends with the same interests and being able to compare findings, one should bear in mind the use of the overseas branches of the family when it comes to collecting information from purely personal sources.

Many thousands of people emigrated from the British Isles over the last century and a half, and, indeed, in the 300 years before that, the majority being Scottish and Irish, in search of a better life in other parts of the English-speaking world. To these more or less voluntary exiles, one must add the result of several centuries of emigration by convicts, explorers, escapers, merchants and those in the Services, together with their families.

The English-speaking races have spread themselves thickly over the face of the earth, and many people of British extraction have either kept close personal ties with the Old Country, or else, driven by some ancestral urge, have returned for visits.

Much material of great value to researchers was taken overseas, for example photographs, diaries, bibles, letters and memoirs. There must be plenty of elderly Americans, Australians, New Zealanders, and above all Canadians, who were born in this country, or whose parents or elder relations were, who are able to remember things first-hand. These may, in turn, be able to provide you with ideas about other contacts, family branches, or which parishes near to the one whose records you are currently researching may be worth investigating.

Do give those contacts a try; the most it will cost is the price of a stamp, and the results could be invaluable. If you are writing to someone with a fairly common surname, or on the off-chance from, say, a telephone directory entry, enclose a stamped addressed envelope. It is always better to write than to ring, as you are both less likely to forget something. Also it lessens the shock of being contacted by a stranger if you have something in writing to ponder over. Three out of four of those approached 'cold' without any proof that they are indeed relations may not bother to answer, but the fourth may prove a real gem, so take a chance.

It is heartening to hear of cases, by no means isolated at that, of family gatherings of members from North America, New Zealand and the United Kingdom, brought about by a chance letter. New interests and friendships, trips and visits may be the result even if no information is obtained. The person written to may not be interested personally in the family (although the majority of English-speakers generally are) but could well pass on your letter to someone else who is. So if you have an address, write now.

Leading repositories for family-history sources

Local Record Offices
The first port of call for aspiring family historians should be one of the local Record Offices, whether it is a County, City or Borough Record Office, or an Archives Office. The contents and organisation of these Offices vary, but they will contain the vast majority of original documents (notably parish registers) relating to the pre-1974 counties and cities, together with copies and indexes of much of their contents. Either the original registers or copies in typescript or on microfilm should be found in the Record Offices in both their present and their former county, together with copies of Roman Catholic and Non-conformist registers, the originals of which either remain with the church, or have been deposited in the Public Record Office in London. Among those sources which one might expect to find in Record Offices should be mentioned:

Parish registers, and their copies; parish records such as Poor Books, Vestry Minutes, Churchwardens' Accounts.
Marriage licences, Bonds and Allegations, and any indexes made of them.
Bishop's Transcripts (copies of parish-register entries for each year and sent off to the relevant bishop).
Quarter Session records.
Some pre-1858 wills.

School, estate, club, factory and other papers.
Maps and Terriers (the latter being land surveys or registers).
Guides and directories to the county and surrounding areas.
Poll Books.
Manorial records (Court Rolls and Books, Relief and Rent
   Rolls).
Copies of the journals of local- and family history societies,
   and publications and transcriptions undertaken by such
   bodies (Tax Returns, Protestation Returns, Censuses etc).
General works on the county.

It should be borne in mind that some local societies are much
more active than others, and, owing to the fact that listing,
transcribing, and similar work is done by volunteers, Record
Offices vary enormously in the amount of material readily
available in printed form which is to be found on the open
shelves.

   A useful booklet, *Record Offices: How to Find Them* by
Jeremy Gibson and Pamela Peskett, covers England, Wales
and Edinburgh, and shows the Record Offices and principal
libraries with some seventy-four town plans. As the Offices are
not always located in the largest towns, and some counties
have more than one Office, this is a valuable guide. It is kept by
most Record Offices and libraries in their local-history
sections, and is obtainable by post from Mr Gibson, Harts
Cottage, Church Hanborough, Oxford OX7 2AB. Mr Gibson
is also the author, compiler and supplier of many other
reasonably priced booklets on family-history sources, and it is
well worth sending for a booklist, enclosing a stamped
addressed envelope of course.

   In the course of research one will probably come across the
term 'Diocesan Record Office' (usually DRO), a repository,
which, as the name suggests, housed all the ecclesiastical
records relating to a diocese. Today the DROs have virtually
all been absorbed into the local County Record Offices,
although places such as Exeter Cathedral Library contain
interesting manorial documents pertaining to manors in
various parts of the country which belong, or used to belong,
to the Bishopric. There are no County or Diocesan Record
Offices in either Scotland or Ireland.

The Public Record Offices

Instead of County, Borough, City or Diocesan Record Offices, Scotland, Northern Ireland and the Irish Republic have Public Record Offices located in their respective capitals. Wales, like England, deposits its archives county by county, and shares the Public Record Office in London.

The English and Welsh Public Record Office (usually abbreviated to PRO) was established by an Act of Parliament in 1838 for the safe-keeping of state records. Entry is by reader's ticket only, with the exception of the Census Room in the Land Registry Building, Portugal Street, where one can be issued with a day pass at the door. Both the reader's ticket and the day pass are free.

The PRO contains several million documents, the earliest of which date from the eleventh century. Generally documents are released for consultation only after thirty years have passed since they were written.

A free leaflet, *Information for Readers,* is issued with the reader's tickets, or sent on request, while several booklets are available on specific topics such as emigration. A publication, *Tracing Your Ancestors in the Public Record Office* (HMSO) by Jane Cox and Timothy Padfield, is available from the PRO and from the Society of Genealogists, or a library.

The Public Record Office consists of two main buildings. The original Victorian one is in Chancery Lane, a modern one in Ruskin Avenue, Kew. Among the Chancery Lane documents, those which are likely to prove of most help and interest to amateur family historians are the Non-conformist registers, most of which have been deposited here. Other treasures include Royal Court Records from the Conquest onwards and those of Chancery, the Exchequer, the Judicial Committee of the Privy Council, the Privy Purse and Privy Seal Offices, the Signet Office, the Assizes and the Lord Chamberlain's Office.

Also housed at Chancery Lane are many manorial Court Rolls, Hundred Rolls, Papal Bulls, Rentals and Surveys, together with the Secretary of State's papers (sixteenth to eighteenth centuries). Census returns for 1841 onwards until 1881 can be found there although the usual place to study them is either at the Land Registry Office or locally in a library or Record Office.

Apart from the aforementioned Non-conformist registers, one should mention foreign registers and birth, marriage and death returns for British citizens abroad; hospital registers for some of the more important London maternity hospitals, and, perhaps the most exciting items of all, at least for the relative beginner, the probate records and original wills and inventories from the Prerogative Court of Canterbury.

A full list of all classes of document to be found in the Chancery Lane building is given in *A Guide to the Contents of the Public Record Office,* volume I.

At Kew are stored records of the government departments and public offices which are not represented at Chancery Lane. Chief examples of these would be the Cabinet, the Treasury, the Admiralty, the Foreign and War Offices, the Board of Trade and the Home and Colonial Offices. For full details see *A Guide to the Contents of the Public Record Office,* volumes II and III.

The Reading Rooms are generally open from 9.30am until 5pm, Monday to Friday, although they are sometimes closed at times, particularly on bank or public holidays and in October for annual stock-taking for two weeks.

The Scottish Record Office is also divided into two parts. The one in Charlotte Square (formerly St George's Church and now the West Register House) holds modern records, principally the records of government departments and the nationalised industries of Scotland, court processes and warrants of legal registers, maps and plans, and the microfilm library of the Scottish Record Office.

The part which will probably be of most interest to family historians is HM General Register House, Princes Street, which is often referred to as the Old Register House. Its main treasures include state papers and administrative records of Scotland before the Union with England in 1707 (including records of the Parliament, Privy Council and Exchequer) together with records of the post-Union Scottish Exchequer, Chancery, Privy Seal and Signet. There are also local records, valuation rolls, church records and notes of gifts and deposits from private archives.

The most helpful items, however, will be the records of wills from the Commissary and Sheriff Courts, the Register of Deeds, the tax records, and the burgh records (some of which list inhabitants and apprenticeship details).

The Scottish administrative system differs in many ways from the English both in function and terminology, so it would be a good idea for non-Scots to do some preliminary work before going to Edinburgh by consulting a specialist work on Scottish ancestry or, better still, by enlisting the help of a Scottish family historian.

A new edition of the *Guide to the Scottish Record Office* is in preparation (late 1985) while a summary of all the Office's holdings may be consulted in the Search Rooms themselves. Both the Old Register House, and the West Register House are open from 9am until 4.45pm, Monday to Friday, and access is by means of a reader's ticket; these are issued without charge on personal application at either Search Room and are valid for one Search Room or both.

The Irish Public Record Offices present a totally different picture from the Scottish and English/Welsh ones. Survival rather than location is the key factor here as thousands of priceless and unrecorded documents perished in the fire of 1922 at the Four Courts, Dublin, during the Troubles. Record Offices exist in both Dublin and Belfast, but there are, as mentioned before, no County Record Offices. Even then, the division of the records stored in each can be a little confusing as the Belfast PRO dates only from 1922 and Partition; therefore many Ulster records remain in Dublin if they were drawn up before that year.

The Public Record Office of the Irish Republic is still in the Four Courts, Dublin 7, where there is a Search Room with a card index system. Among sources available there, are any surviving deposited original wills from 1536 until 1858, together with the proceedings of the Prerogative Court of Armagh which covered all Ireland much in the way that those of Canterbury and York did in England. There are also will abstracts up until 1800; the *Index to Prerogative Wills of Ireland 1536 to 1810* by Sir Arthur Vicars should show if any will ever existed in the first place. Also in the Dublin PRO can be found the Hearth Tax Rolls of 1663, (often known as 'Smoke Silver'), Tithe Composition Applotment Books for all the Irish counties and Protestant Marriage Licence Bonds 1750 to 1845.

Mention should be made of Irish Census returns, pitifully

16

few of which survive compared with England, Scotland and Wales. Early ones were taken locally for economic and religious reasons from the 1630s onwards, and are therefore very fragmented, while some later ones were deliberately destroyed by government order, notably those of 1861 and 1871. The earliest Census which exists for all Ireland is that of 1901, while that of 1911 is the latest available to the general public.

Lastly, the southern Irish PRO holds microfilm copies of many Church of Ireland parish registers, and, while this sounds a good proposition, it should be remembered that the Church of Ireland, being Protestant and a member of the Anglican Communion, represented only about 10 per cent of the Irish people at any time, the rest, of course, being Roman Catholic.

The Four Courts Record Office is open from Monday to Friday, 10am until 5pm; no appointment or reader's ticket is required. A *Short Guide to the Public Record Office* and a *Leaflet on Genealogy* are available by post.

In Belfast, the Public Record Office of Northern Ireland is situated at 66 Balmoral Avenue, Belfast BT9 6NY, and covers the counties of Antrim, Armagh, Derry, Down, Fermanagh and Tyrone. Incidentally, the terms used for this part of Ireland are somewhat controversial; as the citizens of the Republic rightly point out, 'northern Ireland' geographically includes Donegal and Sligo, both of which counties are in the Republic, while the Province of 'Ulster' historically consisted of the six counties listed above plus the two Republican ones of Cavan and Monaghan. Maybe it is safer, then, to refer to the 'Six Counties'.

The same drawbacks face the researcher in Belfast as in Dublin on account of the 1922 fire which took place before Partition and the establishment of the Belfast Office. What do survive, and may be found there, are a card index to existing pedigrees; many family notes; land records, deeds and leases; marriage-settlement details; some wills which survived the Troubles; and microfilm copies of Church of Ireland and Presbyterian parish registers for the Six Counties.

The Belfast Public Record Office produces an excellent series of short guides to its contents, and also separate guides for each county.

Before attempting any visit to an Irish Record Office or repository, then, the researcher would be well advised to establish for certain that the sources which he or she seeks are where he or she expects to find them, or indeed that they even exist today. Unless you are planning to spend time in Ireland anyway, or have some experience of Irish research, you might do well to employ the services of a professional, or at least join a local family-history society.

Registrars' Offices
The last type of major repositories for sources of family history are the local and General Registrars' Offices. The local ones have the obvious advantage of saving the time and expense of a trip to London, Edinburgh, Dublin or Belfast, together with local knowledge and a more personal approach to the area, whereas a trip to the capital, on the other hand, gives you a chance to roam around the Search Room, getting fresh ideas, and also to consult indexes which cover the entire country.

Registrars' Offices hold records of all births, marriages and deaths (together with certain other records such as divorces, adoptions, etc, in the General Registrars' Offices) for their respective areas and countries.

All records of births, marriages and deaths for England and Wales can be found at St Catherine's House (110 Kingsway, London WC2 6JP. Copies of certificates are issued, either on personal application, or by post (for which the fee is twice that payable on personal application).

Civil registration began in England and Wales on 1 July 1837, and, since that date, copies of all entries made in all Offices in the two countries have been required to be sent to London. In theory, therefore, all persons born, married or deceased since 1837 should appear in one or another of the indexes, although very occasionally one finds a mistake or omission.

A visit to St Catherine's House should be planned well in advance as it is not a building in which one would choose to spend too much time, due to the crowded conditions there. Lunch-time in particular should be avoided as at this time the Search Rooms resemble the January sales with everyone grabbing, pulling and snatching at the heavy quarterly ledgers

MY FATHER'S
SISTER-IN-LAW'S
UNCLE WASS
THE GREAT-
UNCLE TO THE
SISTER OF MY
COUSIN JOHN'S
GRAND-
CHILDREN'S
GREAT GREAT
GRANDFATHER.
THERE'S FOR
YOU!

This early twentieth-century Welsh comic post-card illustrates the Celtic tradition of learning one's family tree by heart

arranged on the open shelves. Make sure you know what you are really looking for, or at least what might be helpful, for you may well have to write down everything you can find, and then make some sort of decision about your findings at a later date.

It is important to establish the latest and earliest dates at which it is possible that a certain event took place. Once you have let go of a ledger you are likely to lose it for a quarter of an hour or so to another searcher, so write down anything of interest while you have the chance. It is also important to find out in advance, if possible, the registration district in which the birth, marriage or death is likely to have taken place, and, if you can, the full names of the individuals concerned. When you are confronted with page after page of entries for identical or similar names you will need to know as much as you can in advance. For example, some people are known by their second name all their lives, so it can be very important to have full names, or at least initials.

A copy of a certificate is a costly item (£5.50 at the time of writing, the costs increase fairly regularly); a wrong one even more so. If you are unsure about an entry, why not go away for an hour or so, have a meal or a cup of coffee, and try to do some calculations with dates? When you return perhaps the crowding will have eased, or you will see something that you missed previously. If you are still unsure, but want to try a certificate anyway, fill in the multiple-entry section on the back of the application form.

Unfortunately for English and Welsh family historians, you have to purchase a copy of any certificate in order to see what information it contains, owing to the fact that the entry in the index will only yield up full names, the date, and the registration district in which the event took place. Therefore you are left without mention of parents, spouses or the bereaved until you actually order, pay for and receive the certificate (three or four days later if collected by hand, or up to a month later if sent through the post).

Scottish civil registration records, starting in 1855, are kept at the General Registrar Office for Scotland (New Register House, Edinburgh EH1 3YT). Records available include registers of births, marriages, and deaths from that date, still births from 1939, adoptions from 1930 (listing only people born since 1909) and divorces from 1 May 1984. With a heartening Scottish honesty they also compile a register of neglected entries from 1801 to 1854 and of proven events not entered into the old parish registers from 1553 to 1854; these are kept in the New Register House and record births, baptisms, banns, marriages, deaths and burials which took place between those years.

Other Scottish registers are the marine (from 1855 onwards), air births and deaths (from 1948), Service registers (from 1881), war deaths (1899 onwards), consular records (from 1914), foreign records (from 1860 until 1964), and foreign marriages (from 1947). Full copies may be obtained of all entries except those in the register of still births, which are not released without special permission. Also kept at the New Register House are the Census Enumerators' Transcript Books 1841 to 1891, which are not, unfortunately, indexed.

Admission is restricted to persons aged sixteen years or more, and it is advisable to book a seat in advance. A booking fee is charged; this, however, is deducted from any search fee paid, but is otherwise non-returnable.

In direct contrast to the English and Welsh system, the Scottish authorities make a charge to inspect the indexes, but do not extract payment for consulting the actual certificate; thus there is no need to purchase a copy, and the correctness of one's speculations may be gauged immediately the certificate is produced.

The New Register House is open Monday to Thursday, 9.30am to 4.30pm and Fridays 9.30am to 4pm.

In 1864 an Irish General Registry was established and records were kept there for the whole of Ireland until Partition in 1921. Since 1922 records relating to the Republic have been housed with the Registrar General, Joyce House, 8–11, Lombard Street East, Dublin 2. In addition, some marriage records from 1845 are also kept in Lombard Street East.

Since 1922 records relating to the Six Counties have been in the charge of the Registrar General, Oxford House, 49–55, Chichester Street, Belfast, those from 1864 to 1922 remaining in Dublin.

This may seem quite a preamble, but it does away with the need to keep repeating all the details in the chapters covering the different events of an ancestor's life. The main points to bear in mind are the facts that as a general rule you should approach local repositories and Registrars' Offices in the first instance unless you have plenty of previous information and are planning a trip to London, Edinburgh, Dublin or Belfast in any case. Secondly, as much preparation as possible should be done in advance, as regards both marshalling the facts into as much order as you can, and finding out just what the place you propose to visit has to offer. Thirdly, having checked that the material is owned by a certain Office or library, do make sure that it is in fact available on the dates that you need it. It is not uncommon for parish registers in particular to be out for the making of a transcript. Lastly, establish that the Office will be open when you wish to visit it, whether you need to book a seat or a microfilm reader in advance in order to consult your source, and what its opening hours are including the lunch break. Take a good supply of sharpened pencils (or, better still, a propelling one), as many Offices and libraries quite rightly ban the use of ink in any form.

To sum up, if you're after births, marriages or deaths from the mid-nineteenth century onwards, try the local or national Registrar. For baptisms, marriages and burials (from the 1530s in the most fortunate parishes, later in others) try the County Record Offices in England and Wales, New Register House in Edinburgh, the PRO in Dublin or Belfast for Protestants in Ireland and the parish priest for Catholics in Ireland. English, Welsh and Non-conformist registers are mostly with the PRO in London, but copies of any registers are likely to be held by the appropriate County or Public Record Office, while central libraries are good bets for all sorts of miscellaneous items such as copies of Census returns, guides and directories and background material. With luck, they may also hold copies of parish registers, and thus cut down on the time it will be necessary to spend in a Record Office.

This introduction has been of a general nature; the individual sources themselves will be explored in the following chapters.

2
The Overseas Branches

A glance down the names and addresses on the 'New members and their interests' pages of any family-history-society journal will give an indication of how popular ancestor-hunting has become all over the English-speaking world.

Inhabitants of the New World are probably just as interested in finding their roots as inhabitants of the Old and perhaps even more so. Indeed, one of the transcribers of parish registers for the Oxfordshire Family History Society lives as far away as Shelley, Idaho! Neither should we underestimate the part which family historians in the 'newer' countries may be able to play in the production and preservation of historical material for future generations of researchers. It may seem a platitude to state that what is, in the eyes of a blasé Brit, merely a bit of old rubbish, might well appear as a treasured antique in the view of a less well-endowed American. This is said in by no means a patronising way, and the more respectful attitude is appropriate at a time when so much that is regarded as out of date is lost or destroyed before it manages to become old enough to be valued.

On a more practical level, remember that many family documents have actually emigrated both with and to members of the family and their descendants overseas. These documents range from priceless parish registers and manorial documents taken by the Lord of the Manor to Virginia, say, or Maryland, to the humbler but still fascinating letters, press-cuttings, photographs, greetings cards, wills and diaries which have been treasured for a lifetime and then left to mildew and decay by subsequent generations in some far-away attic.

Not only are such treasures the stuff of which family history is made; they are, in their own small way, the flesh and blood of the history of the newer country, recent enough to those staying behind in Britain, but of pioneer vintage in Australia or Canada.

In the same way, memories and traditions may be kept fresh and flourishing in the Antipodes or across the Atlantic, as sentimental links with 'home' and an older way of life long discarded by the majority of Britons intent on the creation of a 'brave new world' after two World Wars.

Ignore, then, at your peril, the anecdotes of elderly overseas relatives if you wish to hear at first hand a view of what life was like at the turn of the century: Why did their parents or grandparents leave? Were they really such good old days, and was the new life in fact that much better than the old?

A cousin of mine, Mrs Edith Garland of Clearwater, Florida, has regaled me with many a story of her grandfather and my own great-great-grandpa when they were boys together, and their activities in the mid-nineteenth century. She had even heard first-hand accounts of our common ancestor, William Ivings, who was born in 1806 in a remote Oxfordshire parish. According to the American version, the said William was a merry young man-about-parish, into everything and knowing just how and when to enjoy himself to the full. He met his Waterloo, however, when he 'met up with a religious girl, and all his children took after their mother'. An ominous statement if ever I heard one, and very accurate too, as the next generation produced an assorted crop of Baptists and Salvationists as well as a sedate Church of England parish councillor in the next village. I have seen photographic evidence of these worthies for myself and, believe me, there was nothing at all amusing about them. It was well nigh impossible, therefore, to imagine that Father William Ivings could ever have been anything remotely approaching merry! I was wrong though.

Three or more years later, as I was idly reading through an article on morris-dancing because it concerned the parish where the aforesaid William frolicked in Georgian days, my eye was caught by the sixth page which made me sit up and take notice. This is what it said:

The fiddler was named William Irwins and the implication is that he played for the women to dance. The first record of this man is in the Spelsbury transcripts [of the parish registers] where it is consistently spelt Ivings, and occurs at the date of his marriage on 5th November 1829. At the time of the 1841 census he was aged thirty, again assuming a birth date of between 1807 and 1811. Assuming that he did play for the women, he would have been a contemporary and a relative novice at playing for the morris. This, in addition to the more obvious preference for dancing to a pipe and drum because of a more insistent beat to allow the feet to keep better time, was probably a deciding factor in the women having to be "content with the fidler". In a male-dominated milieu such as then existed, it is obvious that the male dancers would have opted for the superior musician when there was a choice.

The original recorder of this information, Cecil Sharp, must have had either bad handwriting or faulty hearing because, as the writer of this article says, the name is always spelt 'Ivings' in the registers. William's date of birth, or rather baptism, 1806, is clearly entered in the registers, and this, not the marriage, is in fact the first mention of our ancestor.

The article also states that some of these energetic young ladies were no better than they should be, for at least two managed to raise broods of children without benefit of either husband or clergy's blessing. I wonder what drew William and his pious Hannah together. The attraction of opposites, we must assume.

I informed some of William and Hannah's Canadian descendants about his prowess as fiddler to a set of female morris-dancers, and this news provoked the guffaws which I had expected, for they too had seen the photographs of William and Hannah's solid Victorian progeny with their equally solid womenfolk. Still, unlikely as a frivolous William seemed to us, the American stories were proved correct. Moral: never belittle the overseas branch!

It is easy to assume that all English-speaking people will have a similar understanding of English history, customs and behaviour. Most family historians from overseas, however, are at quite a disadvantage compared with native ones, even when they have set aside the time and money considered necessary for a trip to Britain.

The main problem, apart from the obvious one of living at such a distance from the sources in this country, is that such researchers lack time, and also experience, through no fault of their own. Added to this the problems which arise when confronted with our dialects, strange opening hours and confusing monetary system (yes, a shilling is now the same as five pence) can turn a pleasure trip into a frustrating and fruitless experience.

To obtain maximum results, or at least give yourself a sporting chance of doing so, it is essential to plan well in advance, and this is true whether you are coming from Auckland or Aylesbury. If you are not prepared, you may end up at the wrong place at the wrong time, or armed with the wrong information. To put in as much groundwork as possible before leaving for Britain and to arm yourself with as many names, dates and comments as is humanly possible; a year would not seem an excessive preparation period.

The most important, indeed essential, information with which to equip yourself is the place of origin of your emigrating ancestor. Ideally this should be the parish, failing this the town, or at the very least the county from which he or she came. In addition, the date and place of embarkation, together with those of the arrival in the new country, are very important indeed, as is his or her approximate date of birth in order to attempt to distinguish him or her from others of the same name. Without a reliable lead as to where the family lived until the said ancestor's departure, research is almost certainly doomed to failure.

Luckily, though, the majority of families will certainly have handed down the fact that the expatriate was proud of his or her place of origin, and possibly spoke some form of dialect, or at least had an accent. Many expatriates were in the habit of boring subsequent generations with their unending boasts about the superiority of Yorkshire or Devon, Aberdeen or Cork, until the younger generations would wonder why they ever left such a heaven on earth in the first place.

Sometimes surnames may seem to offer a clue as to their owners' place of origin. While it is true that, to a certain extent, some names do indeed suggest a particular area or even county (like the Lancashire and Yorkshire ones which end in '-shawe', '-thwaite' or '-bottom' or the instantly recognisable Cornish 'Pen-', 'Pol-' and 'Tre-') the surname trail can be misleading. Hundreds of ancestors must have lived by the brooks, hedges or fields which have given them their names, or have been employed as fletchers, coopers and bakers. Don't forget, either, that Messrs Kent, York and Buckingham must have left home and settled elsewhere before they were afforded such surnames by their new neighbours. Similarly there are probably more Murphys at large today in New York or Melbourne than in Dublin itself. Nevertheless there are still some surnames which can be termed regional and largely confined to one locality, and yours could just be one of them.

When reasonably sure of a county or counties, do make every effort to contact the family-history society there. The Federation of Family History Societies exists to provide information about such groups, and to put interested parties in touch with each other. If you have not already done so, why not join your own local society? The Federation may be contacted at c/o Birmingham and Midland Institute, Margaret Street, Birmingham B3 3BS. At first it may seem pointless to join a local society where you are now living if you have no ancestors from the area, but an exchange of ideas and views, not to mention discoveries, with people in a similar situation should prove a stimulant and everyone can learn from the experiences of others. You may be lucky enough to come across someone who has relatives in the area of Britain in which you are interested, or they may be going there themselves and be able to offer help, advice or warnings after such a visit.

suspected relative of your own before you visit. Then it is time to turn to the 'wants' section of the appropriate local family-history magazine and to peruse it in great detail. Contact anyone who is interested in the same or a similar name to the one you are researching; also people who are working on the same village or parish. They will be delighted to hear from you, and you will be able to offer each other ideas and opinions, even if nothing more develops. Find out, if you can, up-to-date details about the opening times of libraries and Record Offices, and see if you can confirm the whereabouts of the documents you think you will need. As already mentioned, much time and energy can be lost by assuming that the registers, for example, can be consulted at will, whereas in reality they are out being transcribed, or still in their parish and the vicar away on holiday for a month.

On arrival in the United Kingdom, allow yourself plenty of time to do whatever you planned; too many disappointed visitors have had to return with half a story because they did not have time for that extra day in a Record Office, or at St

Catherine's House. Remember that at most places you will have to order copies of certificates and documents, and that you will want to return to collect and check them. Set about obtaining reader's tickets as soon as you arrive; you can never have them too early, and they may not be ready until too late if you trust to luck. People are usually as accommodating as they are allowed to be within the regulations of their jobs, but 'rules is rules', so don't assume you will always be given access to the information you want.

Another point worth making is that the certificates and documents which you wish to consult will not necessarily be as informative as those in your own country. This is particularly true of civil-registration certificates, which are less helpful than those of, for example, New Zealand, Canada or South Africa. Similarly Censuses may start later than you imagined from experience at home. As already noted, priceless Irish documents were destroyed by fire in the Troubles; in addition, the London Custom House was burnt down in 1814, with the loss of both London and provincial records of the ages, places of birth and residence, occupations, etc, of those coming and going from English ports. Lastly, it is worth a try in Britain if you have failed to locate the will of that first ancestor; it is possible that he or she may have still owned land here and that the elusive will was proved in this country and not in the new one as might be expected.

Never forget that official sources are not infalliable, although, to be fair, their compilers did a very thorough job in the vast number of cases. This story from Australia will show what they sometimes had to put up with.

It seems that my cousin's maternal ancestors were French and left Paris during the Franco–Prussian War (1870–71). They arrived in Britain with no trade, and hardly a sentence of English between them, and therefore had to find work as best they could. This involved travelling round the country in casual employment and with no permanent home. The time came, though, when they had a young son and wished to send him to school. The authorities insisted on a birth certificate for the child, but the parents were unable to provide a place of birth as they had no idea of where they had been when the happy event took place. The registrar, seeking to be as helpful as possible, asked them if there was no way in which their memories could be jogged so that they might recall the town or village.

After much consultation they announced that, yes, they did remember something about the place; they had bought an iron there. This was duly produced and examined for clues. The only one was the legend 'Made in Glasgow' stamped on it. My cousin's ancestor was from that day forth legally a Scotsman, even though it was just as likely that he had been born in Grimsby or Penzance. I wonder what would have happened if that iron had been marked 'Made in Taiwan'? Place not your entire trust in documents.

Finally, in the event that the most you can find out is that your ancestor came from the Westcountry or East Anglia, and no amount of searching the Mormon Index (see page 81) yields any more details, don't cancel that trip. Come anyway and see the Old Country and something of what he or she must have seen there. And don't forget either that those newly found or long-established friends and relatives may be just as rewarding as the long-dead variety.

3
The Overseas Branches: A Closer Look

The British are accustomed to meeting overseas visitors who have arrived intent on sniffing out their ancestors with the persistence of tracker-dogs. These eager beavers, normally Americans, at least in the British mind, have become the butt of a little gentle leg-pulling, and it is generally assumed that the majority of visitors from North America and 'Down Under' are in search of their British roots whenever they come for a tour of the United Kingdom. One might almost place ancestors under the heading of 'invisible exports'.

As long ago as 1929, H. V. Morton was able to write, in his book *In Search of Scotland* (Methuen):

> As soon as I saw him I knew that he was embarked on one of those sentimental journeys which happens to all successful Americans. I do not know whether Polish Americans, German Americans, Czecho-Slovakian Americans, Italian Americans or all the other kinds of Americans are to be discovered pervading the churchyards of Europe with an air wistful uncertainty, but I do know that every American with English, Scottish, or Irish blood in him comes back at some time to find his roots. They drift about unlikely towns and villages like prosperous ghouls, poring over old parish registers with expectant fingers and standing for a long time before half-obliterated tombstones. This, I think, is the most lovable trait in the character of the American.

However, in the last decade or so, this image of the sentimental, bumbling but dedicated amateur, usually, as I say, American, has been replaced by that of the methodical, well-informed overseas researcher who keeps up to date with all the latest developments in the world of computers in order to store each precious find, and keep them regimented at his or her fingertips.

The American researchers were soon joined by Canadians, New Zealanders and, above all, Australians, those orderly enthusiasts with their efficiently documented ancestors and their wonderful 'Archer System' of civil registration, which records full details of every Aussie from the cradle to the grave.

If it is felt that much is made in this chapter of Australian family-history research, this may indeed be the case, partly in recognition of that country's bicentenary celebrations in 1988 in commemoration of the arrival of the First Fleet, but mainly because of the great upsurge of interest in the subject there.

In some ways people of British descent seem more conscious of their ancestry than many of their relatives in the United Kingdom. It is quite normal to hear people described as second- or third-generation Americans or Australians, but their British counterparts may, or, more likely, may not, think it worth while mentioning that their mothers were French, or that they have Yugoslav grandparents.

The remainder of this chapter will be devoted to researchers in other English-speaking countries in order to give a taste of the problems and successes experienced by family historians elsewhere. British researchers may be interested in reading about differing opportunities and approaches; in any case, at any moment a letter may drop onto their door-mat from those colonial cousins whom they never knew existed!

When considering the story of how our ancestors managed to spread themselves all over the known world, transported convicts spring to mind, particularly in relation to Australia and, to a lesser extent, America. Firstly, though, let us spare a thought for those who went, if not exactly of their own free will, at least as free men and women, even though they did have their passage paid, and not only to Australia but to Canada and New Zealand too.

By far the most common reason for this voluntary emigration was poverty, generally induced by the series of agricultural depressions at home. Voluntary emigration was sponsored by the Poor Law Unions in a bid to reduce the number of paupers who were a drain on the parish rates. An Emigration Committee was set up in order to regulate the flow of hopeful settlers. The Committee's policy was to mix groups from all parts of Britain so that landlords should not be accused of indulging in wholesale turnouts of their poorer tenantry.

Because these potential emigrants came almost exclusively from the pauper class, incumbents were often put in the same embarrassing position as the Vicar of Chesterton, Oxfordshire, who, in 1844, had to ask the permission of Bicester Poor Law Union in order to purchase certain items defined as basic necessities for emigrants to take with them on the journey. Those Chesterton parishioners who intended to leave were stated to be 'very badly supplied' with these items, which consisted of, for males, 2 good suits of outside clothing, 2 pairs of strong boots or shoes, 8 shirts, 6 pairs of worsted stockings, 3 towels, and a comb and soap; and, for females, a bonnet, a cloak, 2 gowns, 4 flannel petticoats, 8 shifts, 2 pairs of shoes, 6 pairs of stockings, 3 towels, and a comb and soap.

Lists of pauper emigrants under this sponsored emigration scheme are available for consultation at the Public Record Office at Kew (Class MH 12). These normally give occupations and destinations, and are arranged under county and Poor Law Union.

I am indebted to J. S. W. Gibson's article on pauper emigration, which appeared in the *Oxfordshire Family Historian,* volume 2, number 8, Summer 1982, for the above information.

It is clear that these emigration ships became a sort of floating marriage bureau, for those who were so inclined, and, during the course of the long, long voyage, couples would often form an 'attachment', and become engaged by the time they arrived in their adopted country. Presumably some even got married. Thus they had sensibly provided themselves with a partner from a similar background and, with the shared experience of the voyage, were ready for the trials and tribulations of a strange new life on the other side of the world.

Over those long weeks spent on board, as well as marriages being arranged and celebrated, some new colonists even contrived to get themselves born at sea. Custom had it that when such an infant was christened on board, it took the names of both the captain and the ship itself. Obviously some babies were luckier than others in this respect! This tradition could go a long way towards explaining both the supposedly missing baptisms in the family and some of the weird and wonderful middle names which one comes across from time to time.

Births, marriages and deaths which took place at sea should be recorded in registers kept at St Catherine's House, London.

Not all the emigrants, however, were of either baptisable or marriageable age. Some elderly people went out to start a new life, or finish off the years which remained to them with sons and daughters in the New World, in the same pioneer spirit which drives their modern counterparts to fly off to New Zealand or California to see a new arrival in the family.

Australia: settlement and colonisation

On 29 April 1770, a Yorkshireman by the name of Captain James Cook cast anchor off the coast of a 'new' continent. He named his mooring-place Botany Bay, and the territory around it New South Wales. One of his crew members, Sir Joseph Banks, on his arrival back in London, lost no time in pointing out to the Government the advantages of using New South Wales as a penal colony.

This was an idea which much appealed to London. Not only was this country far enough away from Britain for the convenient disposal of convicts on the opposite side of the world; it had the added attraction of being unsettled as yet by any white colonists of any nationality, the more respectable of whom might selfishly object to such an unwelcome influx of new citizens. Furthermore, relations with the American colonies had recently worsened to the extent that they and the Mother Country were on the brink of the American War of Independence. When the United States finally emerged as a separate country, unwilling to continue to accept what were considered to be the dregs of British society, New South Wales must have seemed a godsend.

Pitt announced in Parliament that transportation would be the cheapest way of reducing the convict population in Britain's already overcrowded prisons, and so, on 13 May 1787, the 'First Fleet' duly set out for New South Wales under the command of Captain Arthur Phillips.

After a journey of some eight months, eleven ships landed at Sydney Cove, named after the Secretary of State for the Colonies, Lord Sydney. The first landfall took place on 26 January 1788, a date which has become Australia Day.

These First Fleeters, the first Europeans to settle in

Australia, were made up of 740 officers, 30 women, 13 children and 759 convicts. The conditions which they were forced to endure there were harsh in the extreme, and it is impossible that they all survived to found dynasties; in any case, convicts were not permitted to marry without the express permission of the authorities.

Scottish convicts who left direct were deported from Leith, just outside Edinburgh, but there were thousands of Scots who were taken via English ports. This explains the number of names missing from Scottish convict lists. Even from the earliest years of settlement, though, free emigrants left for Australia, and they left in ever-increasing numbers as the nineteenth century wore on. Two Scotsmen can be credited with the establishment and success of Australia as a sheep-rearing nation: John Hunter, who actually introduced sheep into the country, and the better-known John MacArthur, who went out in 1790 as an army officer.

The First Fleeters were soon followed by the Second and Third Fleets in 1790 and 1791. The main problem encountered when researching those who arrived on board these early ships is that the indents do not indicate place of birth, only that of last residence in the United Kingdom, often a very different matter. Two other problems arise from the high degree of illiteracy among the transportees, a serious impediment to keeping in touch with the folks back home, and, more seriously, the numerous instances of bigamous marriages (albeit blessed by officialdom) when the original spouse was left behind at home, and a second one married in New South Wales.

Needless to say, thousands of couples did remain faithful to each other, even though a world apart, and applications were accepted from convicts' families who wished to join them. These applications are housed with the papers of the Land and Emigration Commission at the Public Record Office's Kew building, (reference CO 386/154) and their details include:

Name under which convicted (not always correct).
Ship on which transported.
Names of all persons included in the application.
Residence.
Sex and marital status.

Children with their sex and whether aged under one or from
one to fourteen.
Name of referee approached, with address and date on which
contacted.
Nature of reply.
Ship on which applicants to travel.
Colony to which they were bound.

New South Wales was not the only part of Australia to
receive convicts. The most notorious destination, and a name
which can still bring a shiver to the minds of most people of
British blood, is Van Dieman's Land, or Tasmania as it is now.
'Tassie' was actually discovered in 1642 by the Dutchman
Abel Tasman, a scout sent out by Anthony van Dieman, on a
voyage of discovery. Tasman, incidentally, also discovered
New Zealand. Nothing much happened for the next century
and a quarter until Cook arrived in 1777, and, in 1802, Van
Dieman's Land was formally claimed for the Crown. The first
settlers arrived in 1803. For the next fifty years Tasmania was
used as a dumping-ground for the most undesirable sort of
convict, unsuitable for Britain and even for New South Wales.
In 1825 it received its independence from New South Wales,
and in 1856 its present name of Tasmania; perhaps 'Dieman's'
and 'Demon's' sounded a little too similar for a new, go-ahead
state. Transportation on a regular basis had already stopped in
1853; nevertheless, it is estimated that one in six Tasmanians
has convict ancestry. Many of these convicts were, however,
exports from the English shires, not hardened city thugs, and
their crimes were suitably rural: poaching, sheep-stealing, that
sort of misdemeanour. A bitter folk-song, 'Van Dieman's
Land', survives to this day in areas of the English countryside,
its origins lying in a London broadside-sheet written in about
1830. Interestingly enough, it also appears in *Folksongs and
Ballads Popular in Ireland*, volume 2 (Ossian Publications,
Cork).
Those with an interest in convict life might care to visit
Copping Colonial Convict Exhibition, which is situated about
25 miles east of Hobart. Another similar place of pilgrimage is
the Isle of the Dead, an island which lies at the entrance to Port
Arthur Bay, where 1,769 convicts lie buried in mass graves,
unrecorded. In addition, there is a series of about 150

enormous gravestones which commemorate families of voluntary settlers – soldiers, seamen and their families for the main part – dating from between 1833 and 1877. Many of these stones were carved by convicts, and they tell a shocking tale of hardship and deprivation.

It has been estimated that, from 1788 and the First Fleeters until the middle of the nineteenth century, about 100,000 convicts went from Britain to Australia. Once there, they formed a ready labour force to be drawn upon by the pioneer settlers who had emigrated of their own free will.

Early settlers received land-grants free of charge if they were either free men, convicts who had completed their sentence, or discharged servicemen. Official recognition of ownership was gained, not by proof of purchase, but by the employment of convicts, together with an undertaking to provide their food and clothing, a scheme which proved quite an incentive with its promise of free land and cheap labour to work it.

Regular transportation to Australia's eastern colonies finished in 1840, with the exception of Tasmania, but continued to Western Australia until 1868, in an attempt to overcome a serious labour shortage there, thus bringing the total of exported Britons up to 168,000 in eighty years.

One of these later exports got her name into the English newspapers nearly 130 years after she left the country. An article in the pages of a Yorkshire newspaper in 1986 included a plea from the Trustee Savings Bank, Norfolk Street, Sheffield, for the descendants or relatives of a certain Mary Larner to come forward. It seems that Mary opened an account with them in 1857. Later the same year she was transported to Australia, convicted of the theft of some bread. The TSB stated that proven relatives could claim the money, which by that time had mounted to an astonishing £1,500 from the original £5 deposited.

An article by Martin Smith in the journal of the Wiltshire Family History Society, in July 1986, makes the point that deserters from the Army and Navy present yet another problem in Australian–British research. Many did not survive long, and in all probability did not found families. About 500 men deserted from various regiments between 1800 and 1850, with the same number again going missing between 1850 and 1865, the majority of whom were never caught, at least by the authorities! The case-history of Mr W. Riedy which follows later in this chapter mentions deserters.

Particular temptations were the gold-rushes, success with which naturally necessitated a drastic change of name and background on the part of the deserter. Australians who suspect that an ancestor might fall into the category of deserter should look through state papers, which list these men, together with their ages, a physical description and their former occupations.

The population of Australia doubled in the decade 1851–61 after gold was discovered in New South Wales. Prospectors poured in from all parts of the globe until, by 1858, there was a grand total of one million Aussies. Another gold-rush in 1882, this time in Western Australia, brought another influx, followed by a steady population increase, until the early years of the present century which was a time of depression and agricultural decline, caused mainly by drought. During this period, large numbers of Australians left for a new life in New Zealand.

Another depression swept Australia in the 1930s, but the post-war years brought an economic boom and with it more immigrants. The 1971 Census showed that, since the end of World War II, some 3 million emigrants had arrived in Australia, from sixty different countries. More than one-third of this total came from Britain (1,024,000) with 66,000 Irish, 30,000 American and 12,800 Canadian arrivals.

Family-history research in Australia

Because British settlement in Australia took place so much later than it did in North America, Australians, and perhaps more so, New Zealanders, are closer to their British and Irish roots, so that today many families in the Old Country are still in touch with their antipodean cousins, the latter branch of the family reaching back only a matter of four generations, if that. Family traditions and stories taken overseas by such emigrants are likely to be remembered more accurately 'Down Under', than in, say, New England or Ontario, if the North American families are long-established in that continent.

The major problems encountered when researching family

history in Australia are, naturally enough, those involving time, distance, and, above all, expense. Once over the initial hurdle of tracing the birth of the first emigrating ancestor – and this in itself is no mean achievement – research techniques will be much the same as those applied by historians living in the United Kingdom.

Fortunately, once they arrived in Australia, immigrants were well-documented, comparatively speaking, as they lived in modern times, many of them well within the scope of civil registration, a time of more accurate records and reports. As in the other English-speaking countries, the Australian registration system is much more informative than we are used to in the United Kingdom. It is also cheaper to obtain copies of such information, and so British certificates must prove a sore disappointment to overseas researchers.

Besides the more obvious sources housed in the various state archives and major libraries, newspaper reports offer a rich fount of information. Communities were small by European and North American standards, and there was a good deal of intermarrying, so that local items – weddings, funerals, scandals, crimes, festivals – were of interest to virtually the entire town. Reports, therefore, tend to be detailed, although, admittedly, this could have been due to a shortage of fresh news, rather than an avid readership!

Specialist publications such as the British *Family Tree Magazine,* the *New Zealand Genealogist* and the *Australian Genealogist* abound. Local family-history societies, as elsewhere, compile their own journals, and as well as the home-grown, these societies operate an exchange system with their counterparts in the United Kingdom and elsewhere.

The Australian Society of Archivists at Canberra has produced *Our Heritage: A Directory to Archives and Manuscript Repositories in Australia,* which describes major holdings and their whereabouts. It can be obtained from the Treasurer, Australian Society of Archivists, (PO Box 83, O'Conner, ACT, Australia 2601).

Australian historians can be proud of the fact that their Society of Genealogists is the largest in the world, with a 1985 membership of 11,105. In recent years its members have been involved in the transcription of memorial inscriptions in the enormous Rookwood Cemetery (formerly known as Haslem's

Creek). Located about 10 miles west of Sydney, it has in excess of one million graves.

Already more than 200,000 inscriptions have been collected and fed into the computer. Transcription is carried out at Sunday meetings, every third week on average, and those taking part arrive bearing bags and baskets laden with the tools of their trade, not to mention packed lunches, looking for all the world as if they were bound for a mass picnic. This ambitious and highly worthwhile enterprise is known as the Bicentennial Project, in honour of Australia's two-hundreth birthday in 1988.

Another exciting venture is the Australian Joint Copying Project (AJCP), the brainchild of the National Library and Sydney's Mitchell Library. The AJCP aims to put onto microfilm all the records held in the UK relating to Australia, New Zealand and the Pacific, most of which are held in the PRO in London.

By the end of November 1986, almost 8,000 reels had been completed; the bulk of the material comprising manuscript official reports, diaries, accounts, lists and memoirs. Handbooks describing the films' contents, as well as copies of the films themselves, are available from the National Library of Australia (Sales and Subscriptions Department, Canberra, ACT, Australia 2600). New Zealand researchers should contact the New Zealand Society of Genealogists. Examples of the above English records relevant to Australia and New Zealand are mentioned in Jane Cox and Timothy Padfield's *Tracing Your Ancestors in the Public Record Office* (PRO Handbook No 19, HMSO).

It is sad to have to mention the weak point of an otherwise excellent system: the Australian Census. No complete sets of returns exist because it is Federal Government policy to destroy them as soon as they have yielded up all the required statistical information for which they were compiled. This idea seems very strange to British, Canadian, American, and, no doubt, Australian researchers who would have benefitted by them. Unfortunately, this is also true of most New Zealand returns, which, apart from 1976 and some local ones, have also perished.

Australian case-history I

Mr and Mrs W. A. Riedy are a retired couple who live at Springwood, up in the Blue Mountains some 50 miles west of Sydney. I give this account of their research more or less verbatim.

'All of our ancestors came from the United Kingdom in the first instance. On my wife's side most of them were felons who were transported for a variety of crimes, ranging from serious (commuted death sentence) to the trivial possession of goods suspected of being stolen. Three of them were "First Fleeters", arriving on board the *Scarborough,* the *Prince of Wales,* and the *Charlotte.* My own predecessors were less colourful, the first arriving with the 57th Regiment of Foot in 1825, the others at various intervals until about 1850. Tracing their history has been, and still is, a thoroughly absorbing historical exercise. No two investigations have been the same.

We are fairly well-provided with information here because of the very nature of our beginnings and there are well-documented records from the very first landing in 1788.

Records of births, deaths, and marriages are readily available in all states and indexes to those records are held in almost all libraries, even the smallest. Copies of the International Genealogical Index are also available in most of the larger libraries, while the state libraries and the Mitchell Library in New South Wales are veritable goldmines of information. In addition, each state has archives which contain records of shipping, arrivals of convicts, Censuses and musters, government correspondence, arrivals of free and assisted settlers, and much more. As you can see, the life of the "white" Australian is almost completely recorded from the year dot.

I'll deal with one Thomas (or possibly James) Gough, who, we were informed, came from Kent in about 1845. Family legend has it that a square in London had been named after the family, and that Thomas had "jumped ship". His father, who was also a Thomas, was reputed to have been a fisherman.

The first task was to look for a marriage certificate as we knew that he had married a Charlotte Mall in Richmond (Australia) in about 1867. This did arouse our first slight misgivings as there was a twenty-two year span between his arrival and his marriage. There was no record of such a marriage in the register, and, without this, we could go neither forwards nor backwards. After months of searching records we finally found that Charlotte's surname was not Mall but Inall. The error had been caused by the flourishing writing which was so evident at that time. It looks wonderful, but can lead to much confusion.

We were on our way now, as we were able to send off to England with at least some information, even though it was scant. Several genealogists, records agents and family-history societies later, we were no further advanced. Then, in some desperation, we wrote to a gentleman in Fairy Meadow, south of Sydney, who holds a fairly comprehensive list of "ship jumpers" and sought his help. Certainly two Goughs were found, but neither of them was ours.

All right, what about a death certificate? Would that give us anything at all which might help? We searched the Births, Deaths and Marriages Index, and found that a Thomas Gough had died in 1891 at the Parramatta Hospital for the Insane. However, when we obtained the certificate, we were faced with the situation that every piece of information such as date of marriage, to whom, children's names, parents' names, etc, was followed by the dreaded word "unknown".

After further discussion we thought the best approach would be to write to Parramatta Hospital to see if they still had records for the period in which Thomas died. Their answer was that all such records were now held in the New South Wales Archives, and so off we went, full of hope.

Alas, all that was available was the Hospital Admission Book which told nothing but the dates of admission of the patients. There was Thomas, admitted on 2 September 1891, but nothing more. By now we were just about defeated and went off home to think about the problem yet again.

It was some weeks later that in general conversation I said to my wife that I had a feeling that the Parramatta Hospital had an annex at Rydalmere, and that it might be worth while to write to them. We did this and, for a small fee, they searched their records, but without success. This seemed to be the end of the road. There did not seem to be any more avenues to explore and so, reluctantly, we put his file away and concentrated on other things.

Some months later mention was made (I think in the magazine *Descent* published by the Society of Australian Genealogists) of another section of the New South Wales Archives situated near Penrith. We telephoned them, and made an appointment to visit.

We were met by a young lady who was one of the most helpful and patient people we have met. Certainly they had records from Parramatta Hospital, we were told, and she trotted out volume after volume of those wonderful old books. We were a little afraid to touch them! Alas, after a full morning of close scrutiny, nothing came forward. We rose to leave, thanked our helper, and had just reached the exit, when she said, "Wait a minute. If he was admitted there should be a record of his treatment in the Doctors' Medical Case Book." Off she went and returned with yet another massive tome.

And there he was! Case Book Number 16 pp 180–1 contained a record of his admission and treatment from the time of admission on 2 September 1891 until his death on 29 September. His death was attributed to "nervous exhaustion".

So that was the end of our search for the history of the poor unwanted man who only lived for forty-six years, married, fathered thirteen children, and died in an asylum, apparently completely discarded by all who knew him.

We continued the search for his ancestors, and at the time of writing are almost convinced that his father was not a fisherman from Kent, but a James Gough who arrived in the colony aboard the *Earl Spencer* in 1812 to serve a life-sentence but who received a conditional pardon and was then free to marry. The ongoing investigation of this case has already taken three years and is still far from completion.'

Australian case-history II
In May 1981 Mrs Joan Saunders was browsing through the National Genealogical Directory when her attention was caught by an advertisement placed by Richard Ratcliffe of Gainsborough, a prominent figure in Lincolnshire family-history circles. He was hoping to receive information on the Tennant family of Long Compton, Warwickshire, and Spelsbury, Oxfordshire.

Joan's maternal grandmother had been Mary Ann Tennant, before her marriage to Tom Burrows, a groom at nearby

Heythrop Park, at Long Compton in 1882. This much Joan knew from Mary Ann's marriage certificate, which also revealed that Mary Ann's father was John Tennant, labourer, and the witnesses Alfred and Sarah Jane Tennant. This was the extent of her knowledge.

Joan was lucky in the extreme to have a chance to make contact with Mr Ratcliffe. Not only is he a family historian of experience and dedication; he is also a friendly and helpful individual. Richard replied to Joan's first letter, and sent her a diagram of his own tree to date, offering to get copies of any certificates which she might need. It was obvious that there was indeed a family connection somewhere along the line, but nothing which sprung immediately to mind, and no indication at this point as to where and when the missing link might be proved.

In June 1981, Joan replied to Richard's letter, telling him something about her own background. Her letter expressed something of her homesickness for her home state of Victoria – she refers to herself as a Victorian – partly because of that state's excellent registry records by means of which she has traced her paternal great-grandparents who came from Cornwall, Somerset and Kent. It is difficult for those of us in Britain who grumble about a trip to London or Edinburgh to envisage a trek of a thousand miles or so, (roughly the distance from Land's End to John O'Groats) in order to do some research.

Joan also included a fine copy of her parents' wedding photograph, which showed her grandparents, taken after the ceremony at St John's Church, Winchester. It was Jessie, her mother, and her father, Ernest Brown, who emigrated to Australia. Jessie died when Joan was only six, and so she was deprived of the opportunity of learning about her immediate ancestors by the usual way of listening and asking questions about them.

In September 1981 Joan informed Richard that her son had just got married, and gave a description of her 'vegie garden'; Richard and Joan were now becoming real people to each other. She also mentioned that her mother was the only member of her family to come to Australia, and that she always wrote home regularly until her death.

Joan received copies of the birth certificates of both Mary

Ann Tennant and Tom Burrows, dated 1858 and 1859 respectively, courtesy of a lady member of the Hampshire Family History Society. Tom's birth was registered in the Shipston on Stour district of Warwickshire, by his mother, and the address was given as Sutton (under Brailes) in that county. Tom's father is described as a cordwainer, or shoemaker, although by the time of Tom's marriage in 1882 he has become a gamekeeper.

By December 1981, Richard had sent details of his Tennant tree to date. In return, Joan sent a copy of Tom's birth certificate, but his parents' marriage had not yet been traced. Joan found it 'very frustrating' doing research long distance, a complaint which is echoed all over North America as well as 'Down Under'. As Joan says, people who help naturally only do what they are specifically asked to do, so one thing does not usually lead to another. Once again she bemoaned the sad fact that she was a thousand miles even from her Aussie roots in Victoria, not to mention her British ones across the other side of the world! Trips to Melbourne were few and far between because, although the cost of petrol was 'reasonable', that of accommodation was 'sky high'. This letter closed with a reference to the traditional turkey and plum pudding on Christmas Day, even though the temperature was 95°F on the day that she was writing.

In February 1982 Richard learned that Joan's local family-history society had just received a copy of the Mormon IGI for the United Kingdom but one of the main problems of getting things sent by sea-mail is that so much of it is already out of date by the time it arrives. However, the IGI does list 'oodles of Gribbles', who turn out to be Joan's paternal grandmother's family from Redruth, Cornwall. Great-grandmother's brother was an Anglican missionary to the Aboriginals of Queensland, and two of his sons were similarly engaged in Western Australia in the early part of last century. In the State Library of Queensland is a book by one of the sons giving an account of his life and work, which gives a very real insight into pioneering adventures undertaken on horseback through mile upon mile of virgin scrubland.

Joan and Richard's letters flew backwards and forwards for another year and more, adding details here and there. In the meantime I myself contacted Richard with reference to his entry about the Tennants of Spelsbury in the Oxfordshire family-history journal, as I was already researching my own family there. Richard had not had much chance to investigate them as the registers at that time were still in this rather remote little parish. It was exceptionally easy to trace Richard's ancestors at Spelsbury and in the neighbouring town of Charlbury where they appear regularly, not only in the parish registers, but also in manorial records and wills. The result was a direct line back to the mid-seventeenth century with a host of earlier Tennant references in the sixteenth.

By now Richard was relatively sure of the connection between his branch and Joan's, but this was difficult to prove as the necessary baptism register remained in a tiny parish on the Warwickshire–Oxfordshire border. There was, however, a slim chance of finding what was needed in the Bishop's Transcripts which are housed at the Worcestershire County Record Office, but Richard was unable to go to Worcester in the foreseeable future. By sheer coincidence, though, I happened to be going there to do some work on the Census, and so I promised, time permitting, to try the Transcripts for the vital baptism.

Unfortunately my time was very limited indeed, with only one bus home and so it was essential that I caught it. I had a mere fifteen minutes research time left, but, wonderful to relate, literally at the eleventh hour I was able to locate that eighteenth-century entry and so offer Joan, through Richard, another hundred years of proven Tennant ancestry, plus, of course, the satisfaction of knowing her true relationship to him.

In April 1984 came the real climax to all this letter-writing and research: Joan's visit to the United Kingdom. She and her husband Bernie, were met at Heathrow Airport by Richard, who then whisked them away to Gainsborough for a week in which they could relax and get to know each other before the research continued in earnest. This started in London at St Catherine's House, where the marriage of Grandpa Tom Burrows' parents in 1855 finally came to light.

Richard took them on a conducted tour of Warwickshire, to Brailes to meet his parents, to next-door Cherington to see a close Burrows relative who produced for their inspection a twelve-bore shotgun which had been owned by Tom himself, and, likely as not, by his father, the cordwainer turned game-keeper. Then on to Long Compton to visit the church where Tom had married Mary Ann Tennant in 1882, and, finally, to Sutton under Brailes where Tom's parents were married in 1855. Further tours of Scotland and Europe followed before the flight home to Brisbane.

Having presented Joan with a whole chunk of history, Richard is now busily engaged in researching Bernie's Derbyshire ancestors, as he too has fallen victim to the family-history bug!

New Zealand: settlement and colonisation

The colonisation of New Zealand can be summed up (very crudely, it's true) as more recent than Australia's, and minus the convicts. Although the country was sighted by Abel Tasman in 1642, trouble with Maori warriors when he attempted to land made him set sail again rather rapidly. In 1769 Cook noticed what was to become New Zealand, but, once again, nothing came of it.

From about 1790 onwards, isolated European settlers appeared, in search of timber, whale and seal meat, and flax. It was not until 1840, however, well after the heyday of transportation, that the land was claimed for Britain by the signing of the controversial Treaty of Waitangi by Captain William Hudson. By the terms of the treaty, the Maoris ceded sovereignty to the Crown in return for which they were promised protection, law and order, and the continued ownership of their ancestral lands for ever. The day of the signing, 6 February, became New Zealand Day, and is celebrated annually by a ceremony at Waitangi.

The first official settlers arrived at Port Nicholson (later Wellington) followed by others throughout the 1840s. Things were by no means easy for them, though, and they found that they had committed themselves to a very hard new life due to the terrain being largely forest and mountain, instead of the arable land which they were used to at home. Nevertheless they set to and made the best of it by establishing sheep-farms.

Gold-rushes in the 1860s in Otago Province, and on the west coast of South Island, attracted thousands of prospectors, many of them from Australia and the United States of

America. The gold-mining booms were short-lived but they did bring to New Zealand much-needed colonists, trade opportunities and a developing economy.

Although of the sixty-three ships which left the United Kingdom in the period 1839–44 only three came from Scotland, large numbers of Scots arrived via English ports, taking with them their own Presbyterian pastors.

One New Zealand city which is of particular interest to Britons is Dunedin, which was founded as a New Edinburgh, by the Lay Association of the Free Church of Scotland. Many of its streets bear well-known Edinburgh names like Princes Street, Hanover Street and Castle Street, and there is even a Water of Leith.

Of those Britons emigrating to New Zealand between 1873 and 1876, the highest percentage per population came from two counties, Cornwall and Oxfordshire, and, from the latter, mainly from the western portion due to enclosure. On the village green at Shipton under Wychwood stands a monument to the 1,429 emigrants who lost their lives when the *Cospatrick* (which left Gravesend for Auckland on 1 September 1874) caught fire and sank in the south Atlantic. No less then seventeen Shipton parishioners perished, and the tragedy is still remembered in communities as far apart as Oxfordshire and the Isle of Bute which also provided emigrants on board the *Cospatrick*. During the years in which New Zealand was being colonised, and gradually building up its own trade and industry, a steady stream of settlers arrived from Australia, attracted by the superior farming and stockbreeding conditions to be found on their smaller neighbour.

Along with Australia and Canada, New Zealand has always remained loyal to Britain and has been ready to send forces to fight alongside British troops in both World Wars. Her losses in World War I were terrible, 17,000, which is the highest percentage per population of all the Allied forces; Australia too, lost heavily, in her case 60,000, followed by a further 34,300 killed in action in World War II, which must represent quite a few missing burial records among the ANZACs.

Family-history research in New Zealand

A large proportion of what can be said about research in Australia is also applicable to New Zealand, and so it will not be repeated here. Although it is fully realised that New Zealand is a separate and independent nation, the two countries have so much in common both historically and geographically as regards their distance from other English-speaking countries that I hope it will be forgiven if I deal more swiftly with New Zealand research than I have done with Australian.

Yet again, it is of the utmost importance to establish the ship on which one's ancestor arrived, the date of landing, and, if at all possible, the exact place from which he or she came in Britain. Unless these can be found, headway will be very difficult indeed, as official records list only those people who emigrated under government sponsorship.

Because there were half a dozen or more ports at which one could enter New Zealand, and as some parts of the country developed more speedily than others, it is advisable to start your search locally, rather than spend time and money going straight to the larger national repositories. Most provincial libraries hold lists of passenger arrivals which appeared in newspapers of the time, where they still survive. Newspaper reports dating from 1842 to 1880 have been indexed by Auckland Public Library. Needless to say, a large number of people moved away from the area in which they settled initially, and so it is useful to acquire a knowledge of the records of each state, as they differ slightly because every state is separate and independent of its fellows.

A civil-registration system was set up in 1848 for white New Zealanders' births and deaths, but registration was not made compulsory until 1855, when marriages were also included. Death certificates are particularly useful in that they have a column in which the length of time in the country should be given; this, if it is reasonably accurate, can indicate the approximate date of arrival, or at least narrow it down a little.

Prior to civil registration, as in other countries, the main sources of information are parish registers, which in New Zealand sometimes go back to the 1820s, occasionally even earlier. Registers have not been deposited in any central

48

repositories such as state archives, and remain in the custody of the various church and chapel authorities. Permission to consult them must be obtained from the appropriate custodian, but some of the earlier Anglican ones have already been placed on microfilm.

As in Australia, New Zealand Censuses are destroyed after serving what is seen as their sole function, that of providing statistical information. Luckily a few local returns have survived, the majority of which are in the care of the National Archives. The nearest substitutes for Census returns are the militia returns made in the 1840s. These list all the able-bodied males of Wellington, while the Colonial Office's 'Blue Books' list both civil servants and, strange combination, criminals!

Members of the New Zealand Society of Genealogists are also busily transcribing gravestones from the 700 or so cemeteries which they have so far visited. Part of the results of their labours have been put onto microfilm and passed to the Genealogical Society of Utah for distribution.

Other sources which may list ancestors include Post Office directories, electoral rolls, and land tenure records, as well as the obvious, more personal ones such as family, school and estate papers, and press-cuttings. An especially useful repository is the Alexander Turnbull Library, PO Box 12349, Wellington North, as is the Auckland Public Library, which is very well stocked with British and Irish material.

The New Zealand Society of Genealogists was founded in 1967 and has a membership of more than 1,300. It publishes its own journal, the *New Zealand Genealogist,* which appears ten times a year. The Society has exchange arrangements with more than fifty other family-history societies in the UK and elsewhere. Furthermore, it holds the distinction of being the first overseas family-history society to become a member of the Federation of Family History Societies. Within the NZSOG exist Irish, Central European and Huguenot Societies, and even a Computer Group. The Society will willingly point enquirers in the direction which their research should take, but it is unable to undertake any actual research itself.

When asked for her observations on the subject of family-history research in New Zealand, Mrs Lucy Marshall, seventeen years editor of the *New Zealand Genealogist,* was most enthusiastic. She stressed that overseas research can be conducted quite successfully from New Zealand. Although she has never been to Britain, she herself has managed to trace branches of her family back to the eighteenth, seventeenth and even sixteenth centuries, in places as varied as Northern Ireland, Cornwall, Essex, London, Leicestershire, Warwickshire, Rutland, Northamptonshire and Lincolnshire!

New Zealand researchers have access to printed indexes in their public libraries, examples of which may be found in the British Index Library, a collection of more than ninety volumes which are part of the holdings of Auckland Public Library. The Library also holds microfilms of much Irish material from the Public Record Offices in both Dublin and Belfast.

Mrs Marshall went on to praise the Mormon Libraries, three of which are to be found in Auckland alone, and which hold the complete set of International Genealogical Index (IGI) microfiches as well as all the Mormons' Scottish records on microfilm. It is also possible to order Census-return films through Mormon libraries.

So successful, in fact, are New Zealand's researchers, said Mrs Marshall, 'that many visitors from the UK are amazed at the experience and knowledge of researchers out here'. Long may it continue!

Canada: settlement and colonisation

Even if we disregard Canada's Viking discoverers, and the voyages of John and Sebastian Cabot, sent out by Henry VII to find the North West Passage, Canada can still claim a long and honourable history. She was the earliest British Dominion, settled seriously after the Seven Years War, 1756–63, between Britain and France, but the story of her individual provinces goes back another century and a half.

In 1763 Quebec fell into the hands of the British, and Canada came under British rule according to the Treaty of Paris. This new situation brought civil servants and administrators to work there, while retired soldiers were granted parcels of land on which to settle.

Something which the vast majority of British people, and, I suspect, quite a few North Americans too, may be unaware of is the fact that some descendants of the Pilgrim Fathers moved on from what is now the United States into Canada, in the early eighteenth century. They thus reinforced the tiny numbers of British fur-traders of the Hudson's Bay Company who were already living among the earlier French settlers.

Canada has been independent since the passing of the British North America Act, by which Upper (Ontario) and Lower Canada (Quebec, Nova Scotia, and New Brunswick) became the Dominion; the other provinces were to join at a later date. In 1931 she became a sovereign state instead of a colony, although she remains in the British Commonwealth of Nations, and acknowledges the Queen as titular head of state.

Over the last two centuries, population increases have been essential in order that such a vast country should survive and prosper, for Canada is second in area only to the USSR. Immigration, therefore, was always encouraged. Apart from the first French and English settlers, and American settlers who wished to remain British, influxes of Scots arrived throughout the eighteenth and nineteenth centuries, the majority of them Highlanders driven from their clan lands so that landlords might turn them into a series of sheep-runs and grouse moors. These were joined by thousands of Irish exiles, fleeing from famine-torn Ireland in the nineteenth century. Canada's Atlantic provinces have markedly Celtic backgrounds, and, for this reason, it is surprising for a British person to learn that their inhabitants are sometimes described as being a little reserved.

It is pleasant to note that Canadians, no matter what their ancestry, are encouraged to take a pride in their ethnic origins, and they retain an almost 'dual' nationality, with the Chinese-Canadians, the German-Canadians, and, of course, the 'Improved Britishers'.

A fleeting glance at the English-speaking provinces, their settlement dates and major ethnic components, will show that the genealogical material available in each will vary considerably from the richness of Ontario sources to the modernity of Saskatchewan and Alberta.

Quebec has not been included in this description because of its French-speaking status. Officially, of course, the whole of Canada is bilingual, as its postage-stamps demonstrate, but it is only in Quebec Province, Prince Edward Island and scattered pockets elsewhere that French really holds its own.

51

This is not to say that French-Canadians are less interested in their ancestry than their English-speaking compatriots; a young lady from Quebec (married to an Englishman, and with sons born in Hong Kong and Saudi Arabia) recently told me that her family know their family history (that is, it has been remembered, not traced, and handed down from generation to generation) from as far back as the early seventeenth century, when her ancestors left Normandy for Canada.

Ontario

In 1610 Henry Hudson sailed into Hudson Bay and claimed the land around it for the British Crown. French settlers were already there, but confined themselves to exploring the shores of the Great Lakes, and the backwoods rivers to the south. The American War of Independence, however, was really the making of Ontario, as it received a flood of pro-British immigrants with the arrival of some 60,000 United Empire Loyalists who arrived after the second Treaty of Paris in 1783. Recently the Canadian authorities decided to commemorate the Loyalists on a stamp. As always, these were bilingual, and labelled 'The Loyalists/Les Loyalistes'; this proved too much for at least one British Columbian lady, for, when I received a letter so stamped, the French part of the inscription had been vigorously scribbled out! Descendants of the Loyalists may be contacted at: The United Empire Loyalists Association of Canada, Dominion Headquarters, 23, Prince Arthur Avenue, Toronto, Ontario M5R 1B2.

Similarly, the British–American War of 1812–14, in reality a series of skirmishes across the border, forged Canada into a real nation, and brought her more settlers, English, Scottish and German soldiers, who stayed on there. Ontario's motto, *Ut incepit fidelis sic permanet*' or 'Loyal she began, loyal she remains', is very accurate.

Other Ontario legacies from the Old World include Orange Day parades on 12 July, and her famous licensing and liquor laws, which range from quite 'dry' areas to severe restrictions in others. These are said to be the outcome of a weakness for 'the gargle' brought over by settlers from Britain and Ireland, although why British Columbia, for instance, should have escaped this menace remains a mystery.

Newfoundland

Despite its name, this is the area which the Vikings could have visited in the tenth and eleventh centuries, and it too received a visit from the Cabots in 1497. The result of this latter investigation was the settling of a few Bristol merchants and fishermen who came to trade in the following century. A further settlement was established in 1583 by Sir Humphrey Gilbert, and by 1796 enough people had made their homes in the province to warrant a Census being taken.

Newfoundland speech is most distinctive in its own peculiar accents and idioms and would remind the British visitor of Irish English, of which it is a relative. Fodor's *Canada 1986* quotes the St John's accent, for example, as pronouncing that city's name as 'Sin Jahn's', with the stress on the last part. To the north of the island the accent is recognisably similar to Dorset or Devon, or at least their seventeenth-century equivalents, but all over Newfoundland Canadians have their own often archaic vocabularies. Their folk-songs have also been recognised as Irish-influenced in part, and most are British imports.

'Newfies' have extra holidays on St Patrick's Day and Orangeman's Day, and on 5 November in celebration of the burning of Guy Fawkes! Other Canadians make the people of Newfoundland the butt of many jokes, some gentle, some rather cruel, perhaps an echo of the Irish jokes to be found in Britain, but written, one suspects, mainly by Irishmen.

New Brunswick

The province of New Brunswick, with its decidedly Hanoverian title, owes its importance to a flood of United Empire Loyalists which arrived there on 11 May 1783. They built themselves a shanty-town which was destined to develop into the city of St John. Many of these newcomers were 'gently born' and must have suffered extreme deprivation on the rude awakening which greeted them on their arrival in Canada. Many of them died, but those who founded families passed on to them all the fortitude and loyalty of their forebears. Originally part of Nova Scotia, New Brunswick was separated from that province in 1784, and given its present name.

Nova Scotia

The French attempted to settle what was to become Nova Scotia as early as the first quarter of the sixteenth century, but with little success.

In 1621 James I and VI granted the province to Sir William Alexander, and the British moved in, or, more accurately, the Scots, and gave it its name of 'New Scotland'.

Nova Scotia provides a couple of strange little anecdotes, the first being that the Esplanade of Edinburgh Castle in Scotland is still legally in that province. The reason for this curiosity is the fact that the aforementioned James, who needed a 'packed' House of Lords, not to speak of extra income, created a series of new baronets with land in Nova Scotia. In order to take formal possession of their lands, these gentlemen were saved the voyage across the Atlantic by their indulgent king who declared that the Esplanade was henceforth to be Nova Scotian territory, an action which has never been reversed. Nova Scotia's second claim to fame is that it was the first colony to have its own flag; it shows St Andrew's saltire, and the red lion of Scotland.

In 1755 those French who had been settled in Nova Scotia for generations were successfully dislodged by the British, who pretended to see them as a security risk, and their lands were planted with Loyalists from New England. In 1763 a Franco-British treaty gave Britain permanent possession of Nova Scotia, and most of Eastern Canada, with the exception of St Pierre and Miquelon, which remain French *départements* to this day.

Prince Edward Island

It is surprising that a place with such a British name should be one of the strongholds of the French language in Canada. The people of the island still speak a reasonable version of eighteenth-century French, despite their own influx of Empire Loyalists who caused it to become a Crown Colony and to be renamed. Other emigrants included a sizeable contingent from the Highlands, many of them admirers of Prince Charles Edward Stuart, no doubt!

British Columbia

What is now the province of British Columbia was probably

sighted by Sir Francis Drake in the course of his search for the North West Passage, but it was not until 1778 that the ubiquitous Captain Cook sailed into what is today Friendly Cove on Vancouver Island, and so became the first white man to set foot in British Columbia. The next few years saw the birth of a flourishing fur trade; then the territory was taken over by Spain, whose claim was immediately challenged by Britain.

In 1792 Spain ceded the entire coast as far as Alaska to Britain, and two years later Captain George Vancouver was dispatched by the Admiralty to claim and survey the new acquisition. In 1821 British Columbia was taken over by the Hudson's Bay Company, who administered it for the next thirty years or so until, in 1849, it handed over all of Vancouver Island to Britain.

The next decade saw a gold-rush when that precious metal was found in the Fraser River in 1858, and more than 30,000 hopefuls headed for British Columbia. Two years later, the Cariboo region also yielded gold, and thousands of people arrived, causing roads and settlements to spring up. In 1887 there was a further series of gold-strikes in the Kootenay area.

Fodor's *Canada 1986* states, not without good reason, that, 'The British Columbians in Victoria share the congenital politeness of their cousins in the Mother Country', which is very nice for us all. Today the Empress Hotel, tea at 4 o'clock in the afternoon, Marks and Spencer's and red London-type buses, all bring a sense of homecoming to the visiting Briton and the 'Improved Britisher' alike. To keep up its Scottish tradition, the University of British Columbia is currently offering a course in Scots Gaelic, complete with cassettes and accompanying book. My cousin's son, his interest stimulated by an 'alphabet' teatowel with the names of certain household objects shown in Gaelic upon it, has just enrolled, which is very appropriate as one of his female ancestors was a 'Black Scot' from Wester Ross.

Manitoba
One of the younger provinces, Manitoba was not founded until 1870, although the English were there in the year 1612 in the person of a certain Captain Thomas Button, and in 1670 King Charles II granted land there to the Hudson's Bay Company to extend its trade in furs.

Saskatchewan

In 1872 the Canadian Government offered free land to anyone who claimed it, and so people came from all over the world to take advantage of the opportunity, thus creating the province of Saskatchewan.

Alberta

This youngest of the Canadian provinces was called Alberta in honour of the Prince Consort. The British had been settled there in small numbers, in a series of forts and trading posts built by the fur-trading companies, but it was not until Victorian times that it grew into anything approaching civilisation. In 1883 the Canadian Pacific Railway reached Calgary, bringing with it navvies, and other workmen and supervisors. Settlers were soon attracted by this new artery.

Alberta's main claim to fame, and no mean one at that, is that it is the home of the legendary 'Mounties', which were founded in 1873.

Canada: Juvenile emigration

Some rather unexpected emigrants, unusual if not actually unique, have been detailed in an article which appeared in *Family Tree Magazine* volume 2 number 6, September/October 1986. Called 'The Home Children', the article is taken from the book of the same name, written by D. Phyllis Harrison of Penticton, BC.

In December 1869 the first consignment of British children arrived at Niagara, Ontario. There were sixty-eight of them, of whom about sixty-five were girls, and the majority were aged between five and eleven years. This form of emigration continued for the next seventy years, and was known as the British Child Emigration Movement, whereby supposedly destitute youngsters were rescued from the workhouse or the streets and found a good home and a new life in Canada.

The whole idea was the brainchild of a Miss Maria Rye who drew up indenture forms for her young charges so that they might work for Canadian farmers in exchange for good homes, training, some schooling, and wages of between one and three dollars a month. The scheme was blessed by the written approval of Canada's first Prime Minister, John A. Macdonald.

In the 1860s the world-famous Thomas Barnardo, then a young medical student, started work at an industrial school in London's East End where street boys were trained. This school had been opened in 1866 by a Miss Annie Macpherson, who also exported children to Canada. Barnardo soon started his own project which included taking advantage of Miss Macpherson's facilities for home-finding. By 1882, though, Dr Barnardo had started doing his own organising and placing, and in the same year the Church of England started to join in this export drive.

By 1930 the number of children sent from Britain to Canada by these organisations had reached at least 100,000, and Phyllis Harrison estimates that there are 1–1½ million of their descendants living today in Canada and the United States.

The luckier ones started off their new life in centres known as 'distribution homes' where they stayed until suitable places were found for them. If the name of the home where an ancestor under research stayed in Canada is known, it is easy to approach the British organisation which ran it, in order to try to find out more of the child's origins. The article gives a list of which homes belonged to which movement, and the current location of their records.

Canada: Mayflower descendants

Apart from its child emigrants, Canada had some other newcomers who may not spring immediately to the British mind, the descendants of Pilgrim Fathers. As most of us know, the Fathers left England in December 1620 on board the *Mayflower*, and landed at Plymouth, Massachusetts. They were 102 persons in all, men, women and children, but it is guessed that about half of them died during that harsh, first winter, of disease, malnutrition and hardship.

In the early 1700s some of the descendants of the survivors emigrated to Canada, where they prospered and founded dynasties the members of which were to be among the first 'real' Canadians.

In 1980, twenty-nine of those thousands of Canadians who have Mayflower Pilgrim blood formed the Canadian Society of Mayflower Descendants, a Chapter of the parent group, the General Association, in Plymouth, Mass. Today, this Canadian Society has about a hundred members who live right across the country from Newfoundland to British Columbia. They keep in touch by means of occasional meetings and newsletters. The Society may be contacted at: 14 Belsize Drive, Toronto, Ontario, M4S 1L4.

Family-history research in Canada

For those Canadians who have more recent or less traceable origins than the Mayflower descendants, family-history research begins at provincial level. Each province has its own arrangements as regards the generating and storage of papers, certificates and other data of interest to researchers. The excitingly named Vital Statistics Acts were passed by the provinces at different dates, depending upon their development, so that, for instance, civil registration began in 1869 in Ontario, but not until 1885 in Alberta. Similarly, church records vary in their dates, beginning in 1812 for Ontario, but as early as 1617 for Quebec, for both Catholics and Protestants.

Like its southerly neighbour, Canada sets great store by the International Genealogical Index, and all the other records which the Mormon Church has to offer, but original Canadian sources, and copies, are to be searched for in the provincial capitals.

Unfortunately, we in Britain do not hear much about what is happening in the field of Canadian family-history research. The British enthusiast will look in vain through an international collection of family-history books for a Canadian publication along the lines of Nick Vine Hall's *Tracing Your Family History in Australia.*

As far as we can tell, Canadian sources appear to be much the same as elsewhere: Censuses, birth, marriage and death certificates, church records, and so on, with, of course, their starting dates varying in the different provinces. Otherwise, Canadians seem to be dependent on Mormon and other American records, or the British (or other European) original sources and their transcripts. It would be interesting to see more Canadian contributions to our own family-history magazines and journals, and to learn of this vast country's triumphs and disasters in this subject.

We do know, however, that Canadians have become very

enthusiastic researchers, as the Ontario Genealogical Society shows. Formed, very patriotically, on St George's Day in 1961, the Society's initial meeting consisted of eleven members; by the end of 1967 this number had risen to 320, including 100 from the United States, and 30 from other parts of Canada. Currently, there are over 4,400 members, in twenty-six branches, all over Ontario.

I have been able to obtain two accounts of Canadians at work on their family history research, one from Ontario, the other, my own cousin, from Victoria, British Columbia.

Both Mr Hankins and Mrs Ivings intend to come back to the United Kingdom to continue their research, and I hope to meet them, and prevail upon them to persuade someone, somewhere in Canada to stop being so modest, and to set to and produce, at the very least, a series of articles about members' personal experiences, and, at best, a full-length book devoted to Canadian sources.

Canadian case-history I
Mrs Mae Ivings of Victoria, British Columbia, is the daughter-in-law of Fred, who wrote the poem 'In Memory of Boyhood Days' reproduced at the end of this chapter, and Cyril, her husband, emigrated to Victoria in the early years of this century. Mae herself is Canadian-born of entirely British extraction. She contacted me in February 1982, after I wrote to Frank Ivings, her brother-in-law, and she herself proved to be an avid family historian.

Mae is in her seventies and is three-quarters English and a quarter Scots by blood. Two of her grandparents were from Sussex, her paternal grandfather from Wiltshire, and the fourth, her paternal grandmother, came from Wester Ross and 'had the Gaelic'. Like so many of her fellow British Columbians, Mae is very conscious of her British heritage. Cyril, taken to Canada at the age of six, has developed into a happy blend of English and Canadian ways. As luck would have it, Mae and I learned of each other's existence in enough time to be able to exchange eighteen months of letters before she and Cyril came to England in the late summer of 1983. In the course of our correspondence and, indeed, after we actually met, I found Mae to be lively, intelligent, and interested in everything and everybody.

Their visit included doing some family-history research, based on a visit which lasted 'all day' to the Mormon Church's library at Salt Lake City, as well as something gleaned from family stories and traditions. Mae knew, for example, that her mother had come from Shoreham in Sussex, as had her grandfather, who had married a girl from nearby Buxted, while great-grandpa was station-master at Buxted. On her father's side, Mae's grandfather was born in Upavon, Wiltshire, and married a Scottish girl of Cameron ancestry. Mae knew too the names and birth-dates of her Scottish great-grandparents.

At this point she had not joined a family-history society, either in Canada or in Britain, neither had she had any assistance with her research so that, on the whole, it consisted of hearsay. She had, though, been to England before and had paid visits to both Sussex and Wiltshire Record Offices, without, it must be said, much success beyond having established her grandparents' dates of birth, and confirming what their parents' names were.

Shoreham churchyard was also duly inspected, and yielded some interesting gravestones; unfortunately Mae was not sure whether or not these belonged to members of her immediate family.

In short, this first visit was not very fruitful from a genealogical point of view, due to the fact that Mae at this stage had more enthusiasm than ability in such matters because of her lack of experience and knowledge of the sources available to her here. Furthermore, she had not been able to do enough preparation in Canada before her visit.

During the time that we were writing to each other Mae took the opportunity of asking advice, finding out useful addresses, joining family-history societies, and generally doing plenty of background reading.

On their second visit to Britain in August 1985, she brought with her all the material that she could lay hands on, and, before setting off for Record Offices, we sat down together to work out a plan of campaign, drawing up outline trees and making up individual case-histories of each ancestor to date.

Then, travelling by way of ancestral villages and a church-crawl of rural Wiltshire, we went to the County Record Office at Trowbridge, in search of long-dead Burdens and Robbins.

We ordered up the principal sources, which turned out to be mainly original parish registers, as, at that time, the number of transcripts was limited. Mae was given a real sense of history when she was able to examine the very registers which her forebears must have seen. Towards the end of our time there we came to the conclusion that there must also have been some Non-conformists in the Burden family in the mid-nineteenth century. Meanwhile, back at the car, Cyril took the opportunity of dropping off to sleep in the sun.

Mae noted everything of potential value, which was practical with a fairly unusual name like Burden. It was sorted out on her return to Oxford and the trees and case-histories were duly brought up to date. We found that we then had two more generations, some interrelated familes, and, perhaps nearly as important, lots of ideas about what to do next. Furthermore, Mae now had a little first-hand experience and made the acquaintance of a genuine original parish register, which, to a studier of microfiches, was a real event! The next step was a return visit to Sussex to chase up the Merrix and Neves families of that county by means of some of the principles which Mae had learned at Trowbridge. These duly produced one grandmother on the 1851 Census, a great-grandmother – Fanny, born at Littlehampton – and two great-uncles killed in action in World War I and commemorated in Lancing Church. Cyril and Mae also noted that there were no relatives listed in the local telephone directory.

They went back to Canada with plenty to sort out and even more to think and talk about. Mae received several answers to the advertisements for help with her Burden research from fellow readers of the Wiltshire Family History Society's Journal. None of these, unfortunately, seemed to be immediately relevant, although one contained information which just might have some link with her husband's family some 300 years ago.

I have recently heard hints that a third visit may well be on the cards. In this case, Mae should be much better prepared, and have more self-confidence; by the time she comes her tree will probably even need some pruning done to it. To conclude, I have long had a suspicion that the British Columbian sense of being so close to Britain, traditionally and emotionally, could, in fact, be a slight disadvantage rather than otherwise. Maybe I only imagined a feeling that the United Kingdom is a sort of genealogical Aladdin's Cave, which, once reached and the password uttered, will immediately reveal its treasures? I should be very interested to learn if Canadians from the other English-speaking provinces, and, indeed, researchers from anywhere else in the countries of British blood-stock, have this faith in the Mother Country.

Canadian case-history II

Frank Hankins of Newmarket, Ontario, wrote an article for the *Oxfordshire Family Historian,* which appeared in volume 3, number 5, Summer 1984. Although he styles himself a 'rank amateur' it is obvious from his writing that he is nothing of the sort!

Frank's family arrived in Canada in 1873 and it was his great-aunt, May Hankins (1867–1967), who stimulated his interest in his lineage. She would talk of how her family had come from Oxford, and how her father had been Secretary to the world-famous Radcliffe Infirmary there. Unhappily, Frank missed his opportunity to ask her more detailed questions as he did not start his research until some ten years after her death. By that time his family had spread all over Canada, and so he had to set to and chase them all up in order to obtain as much information as he possibly could.

Foremost amongst this was a copy of Louisa May's birth certificate dated 12 August 1867, which gave her native parish as Oxford's St Michael at the Northgate, and her father's occupation as Secretary to the Radcliffe, just as she had said. May's father's name was Thomas Hankins, her mother's Mary Horn. Frank then managed to locate the births of all the children of Thomas and Mary, as well as the fact that Thomas hailed from Hampstead in London, and Mary Horn from Cornmarket, the same street in Oxford as St Michael's church is situated in.

At this juncture Frank wrote that a great amount of British research material is available in Canada, foremost being the entries on the IGI, and birth, marriage and death registers. But how frustrating it was having to sit back and wait for replies to one's queries! In the end, Frank decided on a trip to England in 1982.

He spent 'just a short week' in Oxford but managed to get in a visit to St Michael's church, and also to the Radcliffe Infirmary, where, I am glad to relate, he was 'well received' and shown great-grandfather's employment record. Horn's Bakery in Cornmarket, unfortunately, and the house in Broad Street which belonged to his ancestors, were looked for in vain. A visit to Oxford University's Bodleian Library proved the 'high point' of the entire visit, and well worth the 3,500 miles travelled to see its treasures. Frank managed to locate the marriage of Thomas Hankins of Hampstead to a Mary Penson of St Ebbes parish, Oxford, on 28 March 1818, these being his great-great-grandparents. How, we wonder, did they meet?

The name Penson is of interest to Oxford local historians as the family were well-known gardeners in the eighteenth century and gave their name to two separate little streets, both called 'Pensons Gardens'; in addition, two John Pensons were among the clergymen of Oxford at the turn of the nineteenth century, and until mid-century, at St Peter le Bailey and St Thomas's churches respectively.

The University will be pleased to hear that everyone at the Bodleian from 'security guards to the library staff, made an extra effort to assist'.

When Frank went to Hampstead to continue his investigation of the two Thomases, however, things did not go quite so well. He had trouble trying to make an appointment to visit the Secretary of the Parochial Church Council, but in the end managed to find Thomas junior's birth. There he was, Thomas, son of Thomas and Mary, née Penson. He also found the death of Thomas senior stated in the burial register as being at age sixty-six, but, on finding his gravestone, Frank noticed that he was given as being only in his forty-sixth year.

On being approached for his comments on conducting family-history research from the other side of the Atlantic, Frank stated that it was a shock to learn that it is necessary to find out exactly where in Britain one's ancestors came from before being able to make a start. He went on to praise the Toronto FHS for its friendly approach and assistance to newcomers, and for the advice which it gives about sources, both in Canada and in the UK. He added, 'If this sounds like a commercial for the family history societies, it is!'

Although the exact place and date of Thomas senior's birth still remains undiscovered, Frank has found out quite a lot about that gentleman's activities from the year 1803, when he joined the East Middlesex Militia at the age of about sixteen. Five years later we find him with the 76th Regiment of Foot, and then taken as a prisoner-of-war in 1809. By yet another of those strange coincidences which crop up in family-history circles, Frank's wife's great-great-grandfather was also in the '76th' during the Peninsular Wars. Early in 1815, just before Waterloo in fact, Thomas was repatriated; he died in 1832, probably aged forty-six as his gravestone at Hampstead states.

Frank commented that he has mostly 'avoided professional genealogists, for the same reason that I would not hire someone to play a game of golf, or jog a mile for me!', as he puts it. Apart from the thrill of the chase as experienced first hand, he finds it virtually impossible to hand over to a third party all the names and descriptions of all those involved, such as beneficiaries, witnesses and similar persons who should be kept in mind if a thorough search is to be carried out.

He went on to mention pleasant relationships with most Record Offices contacted, in particular the Suffolk County Record Office at Ipswich, who not only answered but also sent off any relevant photocopies with a 'small statement saying I owe them 65p or some other small fee. With faith like that, I return it immediately!'

It should be pointed out here that it can cost much more to actually send off a small amount like 65p than one may realise. I remember that when I needed to send a similar amount to Salt Lake City to pay for some photocopying, I was horrified to learn from my bank that this would cost me something in the region of £3. Luckily, I had by then already been in contact with my American cousin, Edith Garland, who immediately 'underwrote' the sum for me, and even wrote to the Mormon Church saying that she would allow me to run up an account with them which she would willingly settle 'by personal check'.

This is yet another good reason for establishing a working relationship with fellow researchers overseas, as these little loans and kindnesses can be repaid in kind in so many ways such as reciprocal help or a small gift like a calendar at Christmas.

The USA: settlement and colonisation

It would be impossible in a book such as this one to give even an outline of the history and racial composition of such a large and populous country as the United States with its five centuries of settlement, warfare and immigration.

We know from our schooldays that in 1492 Columbus 'sailed the Ocean blue' and came across a new continent. We were probably supposed to learn by heart the names and dates of all the earliest British colonies. The names of many states give an indication of their foundations: Maryland, after Mary Tudor, Virginia, after Elizabeth I, Carolina, after Charles I, and so on, while others show the country from which their first European settlers came, such as Louisiana, or New Mexico.

Everyone has heard of the Pilgrim Fathers who left England in 1620 in search of religious tolerance in the New World, and of those who followed them, some as convicts, others sure that they would find fame and fortune on the other side of the Atlantic. Some managed to do both, as readers of *Moll Flanders* may remember. Transportation came to an end with Independence in the 1770s, and from then onwards the average Briton's knowledge of American history begins to become a little hazy, with Wyatt Earp, Abraham Lincoln and Scarlett O'Hara chasing each other across the stage.

Among those hardy pioneers who won the West and feature in all the best films, there are a few who tend to be overlooked, and these are the Mormon converts who left Britain, as well as the rest of Europe, due to an extensive missionary campaign organised by that church in the decades 1840 to 1870. This was particularly attractive to agricultural labourers when times were hard during the agricultural depressions which hit this country badly last century.

The Mormon Church, or the Church of Latter Day Saints (LDS), was founded in 1830 by Joseph Smith of Fayette, New York. It is obligatory for church members to trace their ancestors and 'seal them into' the Mormon Church, in other words to give them the chance of posthumous baptism as it were.

The Mormons' activities in this field, their amazing nuclear-proof headquarters, library and archives in Salt Lake City and, above all, the world-famous International Genealogical Index, have assured the United States a leading position in the family-history world. The Mormon records and the IGI itself are more fully described in Chapter 4 (Parish Registers).

Although by the end of the eighteenth century the American colonists had run out of patience with the British Government and all its works, and broke with Britain legally and politically, the language ties are still in existence despite Oscar Wilde's observation to the contrary, that the Americans and the English were one people separated by language! Ironically enough, thousands of the descendants of those colonists who could not wait to rid themselves of George III are now completely fascinated by all the sayings and doings of the present Royal Family. I have it on the most impeccable authority that 'Fergie is a cutie, while Di is a real looker'.

In the same way, hordes of American family historians are striving to discover and retie those old, invisible threads of 'Britishness' which once bound their forefathers to the Old Country, and which have continued to unite us in such a special way with Canada, Australia and New Zealand.

One characteristic which sometimes causes raised eyebrows among the British, is the American tendency to perpetuate a particular family Christian name from generation to generation, distinguishing between them by the use of a Roman numeral, as in George Hamilton IV. Does this tradition, one wonders, show a lamentable lack of imagination, or does it demonstrate a commendable form of ancestral loyalty? Similarly, the retention by married American ladies of their maiden name before their husband's surname, thus effectively turning their surname into a 'double-barrelled' one, seems rather affected until one learns that it is quite normal practice, and not pretentious as it would be in the United Kingdom. It is strange to find oneself addressed in this way on an envelope from the States, but, nevertheless, it is certainly an excellent way of commemorating the maternal line.

Good examples of this Britishness which was exported to America (sometimes to survive there while it had died out in Britain) are to be found in differences of spelling, pronunciation and vocabulary which are usually termed Americanisms. These older, exported versions will be met with in older books and documents, as well as in dialect speech of the English provinces, Scotland and Ireland. To cite only one area, New England, as its name suggests, retains cultural ties with the homeland, despite 200 years of independence. In Connecticut, the city of Hartford is pronounced just as it is spelled, in deference to its English counterpart, as is the River Thames, which is not so pleasant to the English ear! The state also sports strong Congregationalist leanings, while its people are of a 'reserved temperament' and 'do not seem to have a perceptible accent', at least according to the *Fodor Guide to New England*.

The same source has it that Massachusetts folks are 'well educated and contentious' as well as being 'deeply rooted in quirky traditions', thanks, one supposes, to all that Mayflower ancestry. New Hampshire-ites are 'taciturn and firm' and live in places named Canterbury, Lincoln, Manchester, Plymouth and Dover, while their neighbours in the Green Mountain State of Vermont have a Manchester as well as a Westminster, Rutland and St Alban's. Maine, true to its Irish and West-country ancestry, can offer Bangor, Belfast, Falmouth, Bideford and Bath. Rhode Island, on the other hand, has Warwick, Bristol, Tiverton and Wakefield, but also Truro Synagogue (1763), which is the oldest in the United States, and has been designated an Historic Site.

Family-history research in the USA

Although research may be profitably begun at local level, in the county or state capital, the National Archives in Washington DC are the place to be for any researcher who has made some progress.

The National Archives, whose contents may be consulted in person, hold those most important of American sources, the Passenger Lists, which are invaluable if it is not certain where the first emigrating ancestor lived in Britain. Lists come in two varieties, Customs Passenger Lists and Immigration Passenger Lists, some of which have been indexed. These two types cover differing years for the same port of entry; for instance, New York Customs Lists cover the years 1820 to 1897, while its Immigration ones cover 1897 to 1942. Only those Lists more than fifty years old are available to the public. The majority date from the 1820s, although Baltimore and Philadelphia have Lists which begin in 1800, while most of them, countrywide, stop in the 1940s and 1950s.

Passenger Lists vary in content, but until the mid-nineteenth century they generally give:

Name, age and sex.
Place of birth, country of origin, and country of immigration.
Occupation.
Last place of residence in native country.
Death, if passenger did not survive the crossing.
Some include the name and address of a relative at home.

American Censuses have been taken every ten years since 1790, half a century before the appearance of the first British one to give details of individuals. One must remember, though, that not all of the present states were in existence at this date. The National Archives hold returns from 1790 to 1870; they also have the 1880 ones on microfilm, and surviving fragments of the 1890 ones. Censuses from 1790 to 1840 show heads of household only, the rest of the family and servants being grouped, unnamed, by age and sex. Those from 1850 to 1890 give the name, age and state or country of birth of each free person listed, and entries become progressively more detailed with each Census. Some of the 1790 returns for the 'Eleven States' have been published by the Federal Government; those of the remaining six were burned during the War of 1812.

Naturalisation records can be an important source of information, giving previous nationalities, and indeed previous names, of emigrant ancestors. The National Archives hold records of District of Columbia court proceedings 1802–1926 and these give age (or date of birth), present nationality and whether or not citizenship was granted. Photocopies and indexes also exist for documents relating to courts held in Maine, Massachusetts, New Hampshire and Rhode Island, 1787–1906.

US Military records are held in the National Archives in the form of enlistments in the Army 1798–1914 and of Volunteers 1775–1903, together with service records, including those of Confederate soldiers. The general information shown for each recruit is his name, age, place of enlistment, regiment or company, and date and reason for discharge (or date of desertion), and, for a volunteer, his rank, unit, term of service and, sometimes, his age, place of joining-up and place of birth.

The Archives hold certain land records, which, in the main, date from 1800 to 1950. No such records are held for the thirteen original states or for Maine, Vermont, West Virginia, Kentucky, Tennessee, Texas or Hawaii, as their land records are all kept in the individual State Archives. Where they still exist, land records are valuable pointers to a settler's whereabouts and subsequent moves.

As in other countries, Americans are usually advised to address any local queries initially to repositories at state or county capitals. Local archives hold church and civil records, and copies and indexes of such items as land grants, where the originals are not deposited, passenger lists, transcripts of British parish registers, plus any published material, and the IGI microfiches.

A case-history from the USA

This account of a family-history researcher from Florida illustrates the results obtained by close co-operation between cousins on either side of the Atlantic. Mrs Edith M. Garland is an almost classic case of the intelligent and well-informed American enthusiast who has done her research diligently in her own country; here is an outline of her disappointments and pleasant surprises.

In her eighties and a widow, Edith is completely British by ancestry although she was actually born in the United States. Her father's family, the Ivings, came from west Oxfordshire, where they had lived for centuries, and her father himself came to the States with the Salvation Army. Her mother's family came from Preston, Lancashire, and from North Wales. Because of the strong Salvationist background on both sides, Edith's parents moved around a lot, but never lost contact with relatives in North America and back 'home' in Oxfordshire.

Edith is well-educated and has had a wide experience of dealing with all types of people. She has been carrying out family-history research for many years now, on and off, but has not been to England since her childhood when, as she clearly remembers, she stayed with her relations in Oxfordshire, played with her grandpa, Walter Ivings, and made herself sick by overindulgence in the 'strawberry-patch'.

The research on which Edith has been engaged has been principally concerned with her husband's family, the Garlands, as well as her own Ivings ancestors, although she had more or less given these up as a bad job when her findings petered out around the beginning of the ninetheenth century with her great-grandpa William, who died in 1894, aged nearly ninety. As far as she knew, the Ivings family had spread itself around North America, while those who had not actually emigrated seemed to have died off over the last few decades.

Since the time when she first became interested in tracing her husband's and her own ancestry, Edith has become a great background reader, and has joined family-history societies; furthermore she subscribes to magazines such as the Mormon *Helper*. She owns copies of all that the Mormon Church has to offer on record of both families, and has consulted Federal and local sources in both Washington and Wisconsin, the state of arrival of husband Herb's English ancestor, John B. Garland. Edith has never managed to establish what the 'B' stands for. In the course of her attempts at 'trailing him down', she has found that he 'showed up in Wisconsin'. Unfortunately for her, she finds that 'research in Wisconsin is always baffling. Either the courthouse burned down or no records were kept or a county split and the records disappeared. Frustrating.'

The only information obtained was that John B. was born in 1817 (no day or month given) and that he hailed from Kent (again, no further information). It is likely, but unproven, that he entered the States by way of New York, probably in 1847. John married an American girl of British ancestry from New York State, in or about 1850, and their first child was born in 1852 in Lomira, Wisconsin. The sources which Edith has had to make do with consist of a little 'reluctant help' from a relative in Milwaukee, 'who suspects a skeleton in the closet'.

The Garlands were rumoured to be among some of the earliest settlers in Wisconsin, but the Mormons, have, according to Edith, 'absolutely nothing' on this particular family. Among the civil records used by Edith were Census returns, and property deeds relating to John's purchase of land at La Crosse, Wisconsin, from the Federal Government, on the land-grant basis. In addition, Edith has a copy of John B.'s death certificate, dated 1863, on which his age is given as forty-six, and the cause of death smallpox. Once again no place of birth other than Kent, and no parentage. Oh for the details of Australian certificates!

A brief attempt has been made to look up concentrations of Garlands in Kent in pre-Census and civil-registration times. Poll Books, for example, showed that it is quite a common surname in that county, particularly in the parishes around the Rivers Thames and Medway. If someone on the spot could be found to help, plenty of further research is possible in the Kent County Record Office, and then John B. Garland would not remain a mystery.

In 1983 I was given Edith's address by a mutual cousin, Mae Ivings, another family-history enthusiast whose experiences are described elsewhere in this chapter. Despite the fact that neither of us had previously known of the other's existence, and despite the age difference, there was an instant rapport as we had so much in common, not the least being a common ancestry as my great-grandfather had been Edith's Grandpa Walter's older brother.

I was able to supply Edith with several generations of Ivings ancestors, stretching back in the direct line to the seventeenth century, while further traces of the family were to be found in the preceding centuries, still in the old ancestral villages that they had occupied until the middle of this one. Off went a bundle of photocopies and charts and trees; 'I felt as though I had won the sweepstakes this week. Buried treasure as far as I'm concerned' was Edith's reaction. Thus she was presented with 'instant ancestors' while I was lucky enough to have first-hand accounts of life-stories and anecdotes of the Ivings family and relatives from 1880 onwards. Fortunately, Edith has an excellent memory and is able to answer virtually all my queries about this period which, together with what she remembers her parents doing and saying, stretches back well over a century and a half. Furthermore, she has kept in touch with three generations of Ivings in three countries.

In conclusion, it is obvious that Edith is very dependent on others by reason of both her age and her geographical situation. She is as satisfied as any family historian (a notoriously difficult-to-please bunch) can ever be with her Ivings family tree.

Words to the wise

No attempt has been made in this chapter to cover in detail the sources available to researchers in each of the countries mentioned. It is hoped, instead, that by giving an outline description of the settlement of each of our family of nations, and snippets of information on what is going on in family-history circles there, a little of the atmosphere of each country will be conveyed to researchers in the others.

The accounts received from 'colonial' family historians should serve to convince any Britishers who are still unconvinced that research is not confined to London and Edinburgh, Dublin, Belfast or Aberystwyth, and that an interest in British ancestry is alive and well in Vancouver and Melbourne, in Wellington and Salt Lake City, even if it is discussed in a different accent. Likewise, if we can convince you that England and Britain are *not* the same, and that Ireland, at least the southern part of it, is no longer British, then things will be coming along nicely!

Footnote

Sometimes an emigrant may leave us something more substantial than just baptism, marriage and death entries in a parish register. Legacies are very nice indeed, but so are letters, diaries and even poems! Here is one written by a cousin of mine who emigrated to Canada in 1912. He is reminiscing about his childhood in the 1870s and '80s in Charlbury, west Oxfordshire. He became the father of Frank and Cyril Ivings who are mentioned elsewhere in this chapter, having married his 'pearl', Ada Nicholls, in 1894, in the 'horse and buggy days', as Frank was to put it.

In Memory of Boyhood Days

I'd like to pen a few lines of my boyhood days,
And I may relate a little of our old-fashioned ways,
Yes, we were an old-fashioned family of five,
And you may be quite sure we kept each other alive.
We had an old-fashioned Father and Mother, you know,
And each one feels proud of them, wherever we go,
And on Saturday knives and shoes I would clean,
On that job you may guess I was never too keen.
I'd want to sneak off and a-birds'-nesting go,
I thought it was all right to play out in the snow,
But those seven pairs of shoes were cleaned – 'twas a rule,
They were put in a line, ready for Sunday School.
And when Sunday came, off we all would go,
And often would tramp three miles through the snow.
Some of those days I will never forget,
Because the memory of so many is with me yet.
I'm glad for those old-fashioned parents we had,
And their great love for us, and the love for their God.
Some nights in the parlour we were all in a ring,
And with the harmonium we God's praise would sing,
When you think how different it all might have been,
If God was left out and indifference crept in.
But, oh how thankful we each one of us feel,
That our old-fashioned parents were so very real.
They brought us all up in the way we should go,
And when we grew up, believed the right way we'd know,
Their old-fashioned Bible they would read every day,
And for God's daily guidance would earnestly pray.
As we grew up and went to different lands,
This naturally upset any of our local plans,
As we pass through all the changes of life.
So along the way we meet fears, and strife,
We often look back on our childhood days,
Which, for myself, I fear there's no cause for praise,
For sometimes, I fear, I was the black sheep of the lot,
But I'm glad that by God I was not forgot,
And all those at home tried to help me do right,
But I found that, on trying, 'twas a daily fight.
Well, when I got older, I married a beautiful girl,
And I thought more of her than of a precious pearl.
For near forty years together we were spared,
But, oh, how quickly the time seemed to fly,
And, with a heavy heart I had to say goodbye.

Sometimes I feel lonely, and heavy at heart,
With me and my treasure having to part.
It's hard to lose loved ones and be left all alone,
But God has promised to give strength to keep fighting on.
Oh, what a meeting indeed that will be,
When all of our loved ones in Glory we see,
And we speak once again of this love here below,
And of how He helped us to conquer each foe.

Dedicated to, and written in memory of, loving parents, sisters and brother, from Fred, F. P. Ivings, January 1943, British Columbia.

Fred's father was Walter Ivings, the brother of my great-grandfather Edmund, and his brother was destined to become Edith Garland's father, 'Jailbird George'.

4
Parish Registers

The Year revolves and I again explore
The simple annals of my parish poor;
What infant-members in my flock appear,
What pairs I bless'd in the departed year;
And who, of old or young, or nymphs or swains,
Are lost to life, its pleasures and its pains.

So wrote the Rev George Crabbe, describing his own parish registers in a poem of the same name which he wrote in 1807.

These registers are the diary of parish life, a diary which, in an ancient parish, may well cover a period of more than 400 years. Registers began in 1538 during the Suppression of the Monasteries under Henry VIII, when Thomas Cromwell issued an injunction to the effect that each parish incumbent was to record all baptisms, marriages and burials which took place in his parish during the year. Few parishes, however, have registers which go back to that date as most of these early records were made on loose paper which was subsequently lost or destroyed.

In 1598 parchment books were made compulsory, and the previous entries, at least from the accession of Elizabeth I in 1558, were to be copied into them. This 'at least' provided a loophole for the idle to leave any entries from 1538 to 1558 well alone, and thus twenty years of family history was often lost for ever. With the commencement of the parchment books, the old loose-leaf entries were usually thrown away, whether they had been copied up or not.

Many of these books list their parish events in the order in which they took place, and so one is forced to plough through entries in which one is not strictly interested in order to find the one required. This is not always such a bad thing if one is prepared to jot down any entry which concerned the family under research, although it is, of course, tiring and time-consuming. Some farsighted writers, however, took the trouble to divide their books into three sections, or at least made some initial attempt to separate baptisms, marriages and burials. Later, some other, less conscientious person would probably come along and start jumbling them up together again. But never mind; the important thing to remember is that one may not have searched all the baptisms, for example, when one has worked one's way through the main listing. There may be one or two more lurking with the marriages or funerals, or even by themselves in a seemingly blank portion of the register.

A good many registers, then, go back at least to the end of the sixteenth century, although you may not be so lucky with every parish that you investigate, as plenty more were lost, destroyed or taken overseas by emigrating lords of the manor. We must not forget either that many parishes are relatively new, dating only from the nineteenth century. In this case it will be necessary to find out which mother-parish covered the area in which you are interested before the construction of the later parish and its church.

The next important date in the history of parish registers is 1642, the outbreak of the first Civil War. Most parishes were involved in some way and many had 'intruded' clergy forced upon them. This was most likely to happen in the years 1649 to 1660, when the Commonwealth period saw a breakdown in the keeping of registers, and the introduction of an official called the Lay Register. Civil marriages were also made legal at this time, and were performed in front of this gentleman, which explains why a considerable number of marriages are missing from the parish registers during this period.

After the Restoration in 1660, things gradually went back to normal; then the entries plod gently along, through the reigns of the later Stuarts, with perhaps a change to a new book at the end of the seventeenth century if the parish could afford it. The next major upheaval was the calendar change of 1752. In this year we decided, way behind the rest of Europe, to adopt the Gregorian Calendar instead of the Julian one. This meant the loss of eleven days, 3–13 September inclusive, so that we fitted in with everybody else. This year also saw the change of New Year's Day from the old one, Lady Day (25 March), to the present 1 January. This explains why one often finds a pre-1752 date (if it falls between 1 January and 25 March) given with two years, for example 23 February 1660/1.

To make a small diversion, here is a nice example of a parish-register entry being used as a form of birth certificate; obviously both the bride herself and the offending newspaper, (the 4 August, 1753 edition of *Jackson's Oxford Journal*) accept baptism as being the same as birth, which can be a misleading assumption. However, read on:

> We hear that the Landlord's daughter of Loudwater, who lately married Mr. Dunsdon, the Higgler, [itinerant purveyor of foodstuffs], aged 84, as mentioned in our last Journal, is highly offended that we should so misrepresent her Age by informing the Publick that she was 23 years old, when peremptorily, on producing the Register Book, she appears to be no more than Nineteen the 7th of September next, Old Stile.
>
> Besides, she solemnly declares that she is better pleased with this old, experienced Cocke than the freshest young Stag in the Kingdom.

So, if anyone is researching the Dunsdon family in the High Wycombe district of Buckinghamshire, no, you have not missed out two generations! To be fair to the *Journal*, it must be said that it still could have been right in its estimate of Mrs Dunsdon's true age as it is by no means unknown for children to be christened at the age of four, which could explain why the writer of the apology says that the lady 'appears to be' rather than 'will be' no more than nineteen on 7 September.

In 1754 an important Act was passed concerning marriages. This was Lord Hardwicke's Marriage Act, which came into effect in 1755. It was designed to tighten up on the existing prerequisites for marriages, and thus prevent clandestine and runaway weddings.

Until this date it had been possible, as it still is in Scotland, and the United States, for a couple to be married in any place which suited them. The obvious example is Gretna but other favourite spots, more surprisingly, were little back-street chapels, and even prisons. According to the Act, marriages were only valid if performed in parish churches, the only exceptions being those of Quakers and Jews.

Family-history researchers should be grateful to Lord Hardwicke, for not only did his Act narrow down the number of places in which marriages could take place, but it also meant that they had to be recorded in a new type of book specially printed for the purpose, with four entries to the page. Thus, from 1755 onwards, we find separate marriage registers, not only with information about which parishes the couple came from and whether banns or licences were involved, but also with the signature or mark of the bride, groom, witnesses and minister. More information about these is given in the chapter on marriage.

Three separate registers finally came into being with George Rose's Act of 1813, and this, together with the terms of the previous Act, explains why one is confronted with a pile of registers, most of which had not been completely filled when their successors began. This is not wanton extravagance, just compliance with the law.

On 1 July 1837 civil registration began in England and Wales (in 1855 for Scotland and 1846 for Ireland) and so, from these dates onwards, it is at least possible to tell a person's exact birth, marriage or death date. In 1837 too, civil marriage became legal once more, and couples were able to opt for getting wed in their own way with a choice of the ceremony in chapel, church, or, instead of either of these, at a Register Office.

The last date of interest to searchers of parish registers and records in general is 1978, the year of the passing of the Parish Registers and Records Measure (taking effect from 1 January 1979). The Measure imposes very strict security precautions upon parishes to ensure that their records are kept in a safe condition away from damp, rats and vandals. Many parishes, in particular the smaller and poorer ones, were just not able to provide this sort of accommodation, and therefore deposited their registers and records in the appropriate County Record Office. Other parishes, perhaps from a certain degree of public-spiritedness, followed suit, and so by far the largest proportion of Welsh and English registers are now lodged in their local County Record Offices.

To establish the whereabouts of an English or Welsh parish register, one should consult *Original Parish Registers in*

A Church of Ireland Baptism Register, 1842/3, from the Parish of Inch, County Wexford, showing similarity to its English counterparts (*Courtesy of Irish Public Record Office*)

[Page 2⁵]

BAPTISMS solemnized in the Parish of _Inch_
in the County of _Wexford._ in the Year One
Thousand Eight Hundred and ~~Forty two~~ & Forty three.

When Baptized.	Child's Christian Name	Parents' Name. Christian.	Surname.	Abode.	Quality, Trade, or Profession.	By whom the Ceremony was Performed.
1842 September 11 No.190	Thomas	Thomas & Ellen	Hall	Kilbegnett	Farmer	RBKing.
November 26 No.191.	James	Anthony & Alice	Manning	Newtown	Farmer	RBKing
Dec.ʳ 18 No.192	Anthony	Anthony & Margaret	Hughes	Solchister	Farmer	RBKing.
January 15 1843. No.193	George	James & Eleanor	Hempenstall	Ashwood	Farmer	RBKing
Feb.ʸ 26 No.194	Anne	Richard & Eliza.	James	Coolgreny	Steward	RBKing
March 26 No.195	William	Richard & Mary	Nicholson	Ashwood	Labourer	RBKing
April 23 No.196	Henry Godkin	Daniel jun.ʳ	Hall	Ballimore	Farmer	RBKing
April 30 No.197.	Jane	Edward & Sarah	Black	Cromcriltton	Farmer	RBKing

79

Record Offices and Libraries and its supplements, which should be found in leading libraries and the CROs. Note should be made of the years covered by the deposited registers as it is possible that the one you need may still be in use in the parish, if it is a very small one.

Scottish registers, which began in 1558 but of which not many survive from that century, are in the New Register House, Edinburgh, and belong to the Church of Scotland. Roman Catholic Scottish registers, as with English and Irish ones, are still with the parish priest in the majority of cases.

When you have decided that you need to search a particular parish's registers, contact the County Record Office, or wherever you believe them to be kept. It is just possible that they may be out being copied, or that an index may be being made from them, both tasks which take years rather than weeks to complete. Similarly, even if you find registers listed as still being in their home parish, do check with the Record Office as the registers may well have been deposited after the supplement listing them appeared; obviously no printed source of information can ever be completely up-to-the-minute.

If the registers are still in the parish, the incumbent is obliged, under the 1978 Measure, to allow access to them; he is also permitted to charge a fee. When making arrangements to visit a parish, give a reasonable period of advance warning of your intended trip. The vicar will have plenty to do without waiting about for a chance visit. Similarly, do not drop in without warning and expect him to produce the registers (and a suitable place to read them in) at the drop of a hat. If you can give fairly precise details of what you want to know, you can write to the vicar for assistance, but never forget to include a stamped addressed envelope for his reply, and do not to be too impatient for the results. Even if the church authorities decline to make a charge, it is only courteous to make a donation towards their funds for the time involved, and as a gesture of thanks.

The situation, though, will probably not arise, as many copies of registers exist, thanks to the hard work of local family-history groups. More and more are being completed every year and finding their way to Record Offices and libraries. Even if you are not able to make a visit to the county in which your ancestors lived, it is worth dropping a line to the local family-history society to ask if they have an index or copies of what you require. Some County Record Offices are willing to help with small-scale enquiries if enough information is given, and a stamped addressed envelope enclosed. Once again, a small charge may be made for the assistance given.

Modern copies are normally provided for consultation in a Record Office in preference to using the originals, fragile and priceless as they are. Again, do not forget to use any indexes in the typed copies, so bypassing unsuitable parishes where at all possible. The copies on the open shelves are likely to be these typed transcripts and will usually have an index if the parish is of any size. This type of transcript has the advantages of being readily available, easily taken down and replaced by several people in turn, easy to read, and cheap to reproduce in several copies. It takes only minutes to consult one, and then it can be either kept out for detailed study or replaced for the next interested person to use. There is no need to make prior arrangements to use a transcript as no microfilm 'reader' is necessary. The only disadvantage is that one can read only what the transcriber saw fit to include. Of late, people engaged in this sort of work have taken to including every scrap of information, but previous transcribers sometimes listed only names, dates and events.

The other type of copy is that recorded on microfilm. This, obviously, gives one the chance to see exactly what appears on the original register, but there are several drawbacks. The main one is that a 'reader' is needed to show the film in the first place, and that means that an advance booking is desirable in the normal way, due to demand. Secondly, more than one person may wish to use the film at the same time; more than one parish may appear on the same film (and, conversely, a large parish may run on to more than one film). Also, the film may well be tiring to the eyes, and the writing difficult, even impossible, for the beginner to decipher, particularly if the original is damaged.

The International Genealogical Index (IGI)

The International Genealogical Index, formerly called the

Computer File Index (CFI), is a list of names and events compiled by the Church of Jesus Christ of Latter Day Saints, or Mormons. The entries are stored in its computer in Salt Lake City, Utah, in a nuclear-proof building made in the side of a mountain! The information has been taken from hundreds of parish registers in Britain and other parts of the world, and is available on microfiche.

These microfiche copies may be read either in Salt Lake City, or at one of the branch libraries of the Mormon Church, all over the world. British branches are in South Kensington, Bristol, Huddersfield, Leicester, Southampton, Sunderland, Belfast and Merthyr Tydfil. There is no need even to visit one of these branch libraries, as many central libraries, Record Offices and family-history societies have invested in microfiche copies of their own areas.

The IGI includes more than 30 million names for the British Isles alone, and these are arranged county by county for England and Ireland, and by country for Scotland and Wales including the former Monmouthshire. To obtain maximum benefit from the index, one needs to know the town and preferably the parish in which the ancestor was active. It is essential to know, or at least find out by process of elimination, the county. The entries are listed alphabetically under surnames, and then chronologically under Christian names. One needs, therefore, a fairly good idea of the date of the event for which one is searching in order to distinguish between people with identical names. Do remember that variations in spelling could involve the use of more than one microfiche, so do not relinquish your reader too soon!

Although the columns into which the fiche is divided include one headed 'type of event', which should include burial, virtually all of the entries are for baptisms, births or marriages, so to be absolutely sure that the person who appears there is indeed the ancestor you are searching for, a check with the registers themselves is needed. Another important fact is that by no means all parishes are included, and therefore the vital entry could remain lurking in some obscure little place which has not had its registers copied in any way.

The use of the IGI may not be any more advantageous than a visit to a Record Office and the use of its own indexes, but at least it offers one a chance to look at a number of parishes together nationwide. One can start off with what one supposes to be the ancestor's native parish, and then extend the search, going over county borders if the need arises, without leaving one's seat. As with any other index, the most useful thing about the IGI is that it constitutes a concentration of the family name, and gives a good idea of the parishes which should be searched, in both familiar and strange counties. Used in conjunction with those publications dealing with the whereabouts of the original registers, the IGI can be very useful, although no copy can ever take the place of the real thing.

Searching an original parish register

Sooner or later you are going to come face to face with an original register, and this can be one of the most exciting, as well as the most frustrating parts of family-history research.

Beginners are bound to have a little trouble with the handwriting of some of the earlier registers; those which date from the sixteenth and seventeenth centuries will probably cause the most headaches. Two books which should come in useful are Hilda E. P. Grieve's *Examples of English Handwriting 1150–1750* (Essex County Record Office) and W. S. B. Buck's *Examples of Handwriting 1550–1650* (Society of Genealogists). Both of these will give you some idea of what to expect and will provide specimen alphabets. In those days writers were much more conventional in their styles than we are today, and once you have mastered one writer you should have little difficulty with his contempories.

Whenever you are doing research into registers it is essential to start with the later ones and the established ancestors, and then work back to the earlier volumes. Apart from being the only way in which one can be positive of making the correct family connection, this method has the added bonus of dealing with the easier registers first, then working backwards to the more difficult, by which time you should have gained some idea of local peculiarities in spelling and pronunciation, dialect speech usually being quite obvious. One also finds out what surnames are to be found in the parish, as they re-occur over the years, and how the name which you are researching is likely to look in writing.

Never be afraid to ask for advice. If none is available before you leave, copy out the troublesome word or words as exactly as possible and try again when you are less tired or more experienced. You will be surprised how soon practice will make perfect if you keep trying; there are bound to be some words which you can read, even if they are only the months, and, by building up an alphabet, you will soon gain both confidence and ability. The best incentive is success with your findings, and you will be very unwilling to leave an entry or a register simply because you cannot read it at the first attempt.

When you do get going, try to note down as many references as are practical within the time that you have to spare. It is tempting, if time is short, to go for the obvious and direct male line. This method usually works, but has the disadvantage that it cuts one off from a large part of the family if one is excluding brothers and sisters. If a slip-up occurs, it may later prove vital to have the entire family together in order to work out branches, generations and family groupings to establish earliest and latest possible dates for, say, a marriage or a death.

In the same way, although a daughter will not carry on the family name, she may well provide a clue by turning up later in another interrelated family, or in a will, so include the females too, if you have the opportunity.

Variants of a surname may or may not prove important. Some are obvious, with just one letter added or deleted, while others may involve a change into what seems at first sight a different name altogether. Local pronunciation may affect spelling from town to town, and may give an indication of different branches of what was once the same family. These variants may cause you to miss a vital entry in an index, especially if they start with another initial letter. Examples from my own family's surname, normally spelled Ivings, are the variations Ivens, Yvynge, Hivens and Evinge, as well as the much more common Evans. Be aware of this likelihood if you do not find an entry which you are fairly certain should be there.

Additional information to be found in parish registers

Apart from the obvious records of baptisms, marriages and burials, a certain amount of detail concerning other aspects of parish life sometimes comes to light on perusing the registers.

Some of the extra writing, to be found between the covers of earlier registers in particular, may be trivial or even somewhat vandalistic, but, nevertheless, can give a glimpse of the writer as an individual. Sometimes he will be the vicar's youngest, practising his pot-hooks, or the church warden trying out various spellings of a name before handing it down to posterity in the register proper. 'Meary', he would try, or maybe 'Marey' or even 'Mary'. Others did quick calculations, signed their autographs, or tested the strength of the ink which they had just mixed, or the sharpness of their quill, by writing a few trial names before they got to grips with the formal entry.

Much more valuable, though, are the lists of parishioners, details of seating arrangements, and of charities and bequests known as 'Briefs' which were parish collections made for deserving causes at home and overseas. These gave the amount which each person contributed. Other lists are of confirmation candidates, with their ages; officers elected for parish duties; and even, in two or three rare cases, Protestation Returns (see Chapter 8).

A fairly modern register from Wolvercote, Oxford, has a list of communicants for the beginning of the present century, among whom were, for 1904, 'Fluffy', 'German lady', 'strange lady, large nose', 'stout young lady', and 'red-haired girl's friend'; for 1906, 'unknown regular girl' and 'grey-haired strong lady'; for 1908, 'Mr and Mrs Pseudo Baldhead'; and for 1909, 'Tosher in blazer and Mrs Tosher'. It is a pity that the identity of these people must remain lost for ever; on the other hand, as the descriptions are somewhat personal, maybe this is not such a bad thing after all!

Bishops' Transcripts

Lastly, one should mention some rather hybrid documents which are related to parish registers, but are also copies of them. These are the Bishops' Transcripts, usually abbreviated to BTs.

These transcripts were copies of the registers' entries; they were made annually and submitted to the bishop within one month of Easter. This was done in accordance with instructions given in 1598. Bishops' Transcripts take the form, in the earlier editions, of folded or rolled pieces of vellum; they look a little like treasure maps, which indeed they can sometimes prove to be. Later Transcripts were filled in on properly printed forms.

Like the registers themselves, Transcripts vary according to the writer, his artistic talents, and his sense of duty concerning these matters. Where it was too much trouble for the incumbent or his clerk to make a record of parish events neatly and efficiently in the first place, it was certainly too much effort to make a good transcription, and, together with a certain amount of carelessness on the part of the episcopal staff, this means that many BTs are faulty or missing.

The Transcripts are not always to be found in the same Record Office as the original registers. They were sent in to the Diocesan – as opposed to the County – Record Office, which may not necessarily be the same place. For example, a parish may lie in one county, but in a diocese which is centred in a neighbouring one. A certain tiny parish in which I am interested started off life in Berkshire, but was switched to Oxfordshire with the county-boundary changes of 1974. The register collection remains with Berkshire, with copies made for Oxfordshire CRO, but here is the confusion: the BTs are to be found in the Wiltshire CRO at Trowbridge. Why? Because the parish lies within the diocese of Salisbury!

Nevertheless it is well worth trying the BTs if the registers are damaged, missing or illegible for the period in question. This is particularly true of the mid-seventeenth century with all its disruptions.

5
Birth and Baptism

Two points should be kept in mind when consulting birth and baptism records. The first is that the date or even the year of baptism is not necessarily the same as the date of birth. In the vast majority of cases, of course, baptism took place within weeks if not days of birth, but it is by no means unknown to find quite old children or even adults being christened, particularly if they have been accepted into the Church from another religion or denomination.

The second thing to remember is that the seemingly ideal ancestor just might have died before he or she was old enough to marry and produce descendants; so, if possible, baptism and burial records should be used in conjunction, in order to at least attempt to discover if the infant of the name and date which you are searching for did indeed survive long enough to become your ancestor. Beware of two (or more!) brothers, sisters or cousins with identical names.

Having spoken of later baptisms, one will promptly find plenty of entries which record birth, baptism and even death on the same day, occasionally coupled with the name of the mother who died in or after childbirth. There is an element of resignation to the will of God; the death of a woman in childbirth was considered to be almost an occupational hazard. The mothers themselves, and therefore the babies too, were often in poor health from disease and malnutrition, too young for childbearing, or else worn out by a constant string of pregnancies. Birth was a risky business for both mother and child, until well into the present century. The surroundings were not always very suitable, as this entry, dated 5 January 1580–1, from the Priory Church of Great Malvern shows: 'Joan daughter of a certain vagrant woman delivered in the barne of Thomas Needs of Housell.' More comfortable but still tragic, was the following entry, dated 28 March, 1557, from the same parish: 'Fruancis Harryell son of Richard at

EXTRACT ENTRY OF BIRTH: 17 & 18 Victoriæ Cap. 80, § 37.

No.	(1) Name and Surname.	(2) When and Where Born.	(3) Sex.	(4) Name, Surname, and Rank or Profession of Father. Name, and Maiden Surname of Mother. Date and Place of Marriage.	(5) Signature and Qualification of Informant, and Residence, if out of the House in which the Birth occurred.	(6) When and Where Registered, and Signature of Registrar.
1084	John Derrick Brown	1936, June First 9h. 10m. A.M. Queen Mary Maternity Home. Edinburgh	M	John Christie Brown Medical Officer (Registrar-General's Department) (Usual Residence 57 Broadswall, Leith, Edinburgh) Nina Mary Stewart Brown M.S. Brooks 1930 November 1st Edinburgh	(Signed) John C. Brown Father	1936, June 17th At Edinburgh (Signed) H. M. Mitchell Asst. Registrar. (Initd.) R.D.R.

EXTRACTED from the REGISTER BOOK OF BIRTHS, for the _District_ of _George Square_, in the _City_ of _Edinburgh_ this _Seventeenth_ day of _June_ Nineteen Hundred and _thirty-six_. _Margaret Steel Asst. Registrar._

A Scottish Birth Certificate; note that the date and place of the parents' marriage is shown in column 5, a detail which is missing from English and Welsh certificates (*Courtesy of Mr J. D. Brown*) home by the midwife and buryed the same day.'

Those of us who are living at the end of the twentieth century tend to deceive ourselves by imagining that all this giving birth in barns, and being born or dying by the wayside was one of the nastier aspects of our ancestors' lives, which we, superior beings, have risen above, and that such stories are scarcely applicable to us today. Unhappily this is not at all the case, as the following account, which appeared in the *Oxford Journal* shortly before Christmas 1986, shows:

> The dead baby girl found dumped on the side of the road will be given a decent funeral . . . even though no one knows who she is. Despite intensive investigations, the mother couldn't be found, and the local authority will be paying for a cremation.

Coroner Nicholas Gardiner heard at an Oxford inquest the body had been lying by the Burford to Charlbury road for some time, and was decomposed. Mr Gardiner went through the formalities of reading the evidence to an empty courtroom.

Illegitimacy

This is a subject which many people avoid noting in their family annals, and, in extreme cases, it can cause the more sensitive to give up the search altogether. The stigma of illegitimate birth has, thank goodness, all but disappeared in Britain, but this is a very recent development. However it was described or regarded, illegitimacy was a very common condition throughout the country, obvious enough for mention of it to find its way into Crabbe's poem, 'The Parish Register':

> With evil omen we that year begin:
> A child of Shame—stern Justice adds, of Sin—
> Is first recorded; I would hide the deed,
> But vain the wish; I sigh and I proceed:
> And could I well th' instructive truth convey,
> 'Twould warn the giddy and awake the gay.

Vicars did, in fact, have various methods by which they either revealed or concealed that the child whose baptism they were recording was illegitimate. These ranged from the bald description 'bastard' or 'spurious', improving slightly with 'fatherless child' or 'of husbandless mother' or 'single woman'. Sometimes a vicar will resort to Latin and write 'fil. pop. ex rep. pat. X et Y', even when the register has been kept in English for many years. The best of a bad bunch would appear to be 'love child', and let us hope that this is just what they were. Another indication of illegitimacy was the use of two surnames joined by the word 'alias', as in 'John Jones alias Smith', using the surnames of both parents. Thus at Church Eaton, Staffordshire, an entry for 25 December 1585 reads: 'John son of Margerie Giyllam alias Lonne, base born, and the son of Robert Storie as she sayth.' History seems to have repeated itself in that particular family.

The use of the term 'alias', however, does not automatically imply bastardy. It was sometimes used of an adopted child, or one whose mother remarried. Sometimes it is used also as a kind of trade name, in which the name of the master at one's place of occupation (usually for an apprentice), a place-name, or the maiden name of the mother (as in the United States today), is added, thus turning the surname into a double-barrelled one.

We are accustomed to think of the permissive society as a recent phenomenon as if we had invented it ourselves, but it came a few centuries previously, at least to rural Warwickshire, as the registers of the little parish of Wolfhamcote show. On 24 March 1689 a certain Thomas Bucknell married Katherine Shaw. On 21 July of the same year Thomas and Katherine's son, Robert, was baptised. This seems fair enough until we read another entry for the very same day, also a baptism: 'Bucknell Whood son of Thomas Bucknill and Rebecka Whood, spurious, born at Salbridge.' One wonders how Thomas made up his mind which of his pregnant girlfriends to marry. It seems surprising that Rebecka was forgiving enough to name her little son after Thomas; or maybe she was determined to shame him. At least the child was acknowledged and baptised.

An act of 1732–3 stated that a pregnant woman who was due to give birth to an illegitimate child must declare the fact, and also reveal the name of the father. An increase in illegitimacy during the eighteenth century made parish officers attempt to force the respective parents to marry if this were possible. This procedure would save the cost of taking the father to court in order to make sure that he shouldered his responsibilities, although there was always the danger of the whole family becoming a burden on the parish. If no father was forthcoming, or the woman concealed his name, the mother's parish was liable for the child's upkeep, hence the concern, economic as much as moral, perhaps.

The alternative to marriage, or being kept by the parish entirely, was the extraction of a sum of money from the father, either in a lump sum or a series of payments over a period of time for the maintainance of the child. This arrangement was sealed by means of a Bond of Idemnification, which, in turn, produced a document called a Bastardy Bond. Those bonds which survive are usually kept with the parish registers and other parish records, either in the parish itself or in the County Record Office.

Occasionally the practice of taking an unmarried mother-to-be in front of a magistrate backfired on the parish officer involved, at least if this report in a newspaper from 1764 is at all typical:

A few days ago a Parish Officer of Coggs near Witney in this County [Oxfordshire] whose watchfulness to prevent his Parish from being burthened, together with a conscientious regard for the due discharge of his Office, had obliged him to bring a pregnant unmarried woman to this City [Oxford] for examination before a Magistrate, found his case but ill-rewarded. For, after taking instructions from a Surrogate, and surmounting many obstacles, having at length with some difficulty found a justice, she had the confidence to swear her big Belly upon our industrious Parish Officer, and was even so circumstantial as to fix upon the time and Place. It seems he is far from being a young man, and, what renders the incident rather more perplexing, has a family of Children and wife now living.

By the latter years of the eighteenth century, a straightforward attitude to illegitimacy and adoption seems to have developed, according to this advertisement, dated 6 June 1778:

For the benefit of Married and Unmarried Ladies:

An eminent Man-Midwife, from a real tenderness of Heart and a thorough conviction of the Utility of his plan, has at great expense fitted up a compleat house for the reception of those ladies who are so situated as not to have the convenience of lying-in at their own houses.

They will be treated with great care and tenderness and have all necessaries found them, the child will be taken care of after the month if required.

For particulars apply by line (post paid)

In short, then, illegitimate ancestors are hardly uncommon; in fact in some parishes, rural ones mainly, the practice seems to have been acceptable, especially in the eighteenth century. There is no reason why it should prove an obstacle to family-history research (unless, of course, the father's name is not recorded, in which case that branch of the family must remain anonymous for ever). Legitimate or not, the blood strain remains the same, even if the name is continued through the female line for a generation or two.

Baptism

The baptism of a first-born child, and sometimes of subsequent ones, may be difficult to trace in the couple's home parish. It may well turn out that the event took place in the mother's ancestral or home parish if this is different from the one in which they lived later. Then, as now, girls often went home to Mum for their confinements, and this is particularly likely for the first. Even when hospitals came into general use, only those who lived too far away from their relatives or friends for them to help out (for instance orphans or newcomers to a town) would have dreamed of being among strangers for such an important occasion. So, until about a generation ago, nearly everyone was born in the family home.

If the baptismal entry is not to be found in the marital or parental parish, the IGI or a family-history society Marriage Index may come into its own. For sentimental reasons families sometimes preferred to have their children christened where previous generations of the family had been baptised. With an Index one can see at a glance any parish favoured by the family from the sixteenth century onwards. This may, or may not, be near the place where they actually lived at the time of the christening.

In earlier times babies were christened as soon as practicable after birth, usually within a few days in case they should not survive. The period grew to a few weeks, and then to the two or three months which is the usual interval today between birth and baptism. Some parents, however, seem to have gone in for joint and even 'mass' christening, sometimes with cousins being baptised together. There is, of course, the possibility of twins, or even triplets, but this is usually noted. When one gets an entry such as this one from Bampton, Oxfordshire, in 1672, 'Ivings, Jacob, James, Elizabeth and Mary, all of Robert', it seems certain that the participants were all of different ages. Sometimes, rather infrequently admittedly, one even finds entire families baptised together: father, mother and maybe up to six children. It would seem likely that these entries relate to former Non-conformists, probably Baptists who would not have been christened in infancy, who have all come together into the Anglican fold.

When checking on the baptism of my maternal grandmother in 1880, I chanced upon a joint baptismal entry for November 1884: 'Fry, Edith Sarah and Jane May, were baptised privately in their own home.' Baptism at home was not so very uncommon, as sickly children were sometimes christened at birth for fear that they might not live long enough for the conventional gap between birth and baptism. What did make me smile, though (and, if I had not been in Oxford University's silent and scholarly Bodleian Library at that moment I should definitely have allowed myself a laugh out loud), was the knowledge that both of the above twins did indeed outlive the expectations of the vicar. They were my aforementioned grandmother's first cousins. She died of tuberculosis at the early age of forty-one, but, of those sickly infants, one lived to ninety-nine while the survivor did not succumb until she had made her century!

Baptisms not taking place in a parish church

If it seems at all likely that the ancestor you are researching could have been baptised outside the Church of England, it may be worth while exploring the possibility that the parents may have been Non-conformist or Roman Catholic, even if former and subsequent generations show no sign of being so. Alternately they may have been in London, in prison or even abroad.

Roman Catholic parish registers remain with the parish priest, while the majority of Non-conformist ones have been deposited in the Public Record Office in Chancery Lane. Remember to check whether copies have been made and given to the county's central library or County Record Office, or to the local church or chapel, before you set off to London. The period in which you are interested may be covered by the register which is still in use, so try locally first.

If you suspect that the family strayed further afield, a visit to the PRO may prove of interest as it holds birth and/or baptism records for the Chelsea Hospital (for 1691 to 1812), and the Foundling, and British Lying-In Hospitals, as well as those of the Fleet and King's Bench Prisons.

St Catherine's House in London's Kingsway can offer even more exotic locations as it holds Chaplains Abroad records from 1796 to 1880 (from 1881 these are kept by Command Headquarters but St Catherine's House holds copies). Here are also to be found some regimental registers 1790–1924 and details of births on Royal Navy vessels since 1837, and those on merchant ships between 1837 and 1874. For 1875 onwards, application should be made to the Registrar General for Shipping and Seamen, Llandaff, Cardiff. Lastly, St Catherine's House also has records of baptisms 1720–1856 in a rather unlikely sounding place, the Greenwich Hospital for Navy Pensioners. One presumes that the fathers were either invalided out of the service or were on the staff!

Names

Even if you meet with little or no success in finding your quarry, you are sure to come across some new and fascinating names: old ones which died out with Dickens, regional variations on old favourites, and highly inappropriate biblical names, often spelt in the most novel and appealing ways.

How, we wonder, could anyone possibly call a newborn babe Elijah or Ebeneezer, or even Marmaduke or Amos? And whatever were the seventeenth-century Cornish parents Mr and Mrs Ching thinking about when they called their son

Nabucadnezer, or Mr and Mrs Burt when they called theirs Bezaleel, he who grew up to become the Minister of Landulph? In the same county, how about Hopson Baby when he himself had children, or Angell Angell, the young Cockney bride? Worse still, how about poor little illegitimate Chastity?

With some names it is a little difficult to even be sure of which gender the bearer was. Unlike today, Christians and Juliens were girls, as were Emmetts (a dialect word for ant!) and Parnells, a diminutive of Petronella. Another puzzler is Fridsweed (feminine) found at Woodstock, Oxfordshire, until one realises that Frideswide is the patron saint of Oxford, and that Fridsweed is nearer the original Anglo-Saxon pronunciation than today's version.

Other problems can be caused by the Latinisation of some Christian names, most of which, however, will cause little or no confusion. Henricus, Ricardus or Maria are obvious enough, Johannes, Guillielmus and Petrus turn fairly neatly into John, William and Peter, but how can one be sure whether Jacobus is Jacob, when he could equally well be James in disguise; also is Johanna to be translated as Jane or Joan?

Something which will seem strange to the modern researcher is our ancestors' tendency to christen two, or occasionally more, children with the same name. It is not uncommon to find the first three baptised with a name which was obviously important to the family. Usually, on turning to the burials, one finds that numbers 2 and 3 are replacements for deceased brothers and sisters, but sometimes both or all lived. Then, one wonders, what nicknames were used to distinguish one William from another: Will and Bill? It must also have been a little tricky differentiating between grandfather, father, uncle, cousin and son (not to mention grandsons) all named Henry.

In the autumn 1982 edition of the *Oxford Family Historian* there appeared an interesting article by Mr E. Eustace, entitled 'Names Below Stairs'. In it the author tells us how sometimes an employer would insist on a change of name, if the real one was disapproved of by the family. The chief reasons for disapproval, it would seem, were servants bearing names already belonging to a member of the employer's family, or ones which were deemed pretentious. On occasions even the surname met with disfavour and was forcibly changed.

Some employers regimented their staff to the extent that they matched certain names to certain positions; thus the cook might always be called Mary, the parlour-maid Jane, and so on, regardless of their given names at baptism. This custom, fortunately not too frequently practised, would play havoc with the correlation of baptismal entries, birth certificates and Census returns.

Civil registration

Nearly everybody will have had some experience of birth certificates if only their own. Civil registration began in England and Wales on 1 July 1837 (though it did not become compulsory until 1875) and, since that date, copies of all entries made by registrars throughout these two countries have had to be sent to the General Register Office at St Catherine's House (110 Kingsway, London WC2 6JP). Anglo-Welsh birth certificates give the following information:

Place of birth.
Names of parents, their address and the occupation of the father.
Maiden name of the mother.
Name of the person who furnished the information (generally one of the parents).

Certificates may be purchased either from St Catherine's House, or locally on application to the registrar who registered the birth, although this latter only applies to the certificates ordered at the time of registration or very shortly afterwards until the current register is filled up. It is possible, however, to obtain either a standard certificate or a short one (not normally much use for historical purposes) from the Superintendent Registrar of the area. A general search in the indexes to the registers is also available on payment of a fee.

Scottish civil registration began in 1855 when a form of pilot scheme was introduced. Certificates for this year only are much more detailed than those for subsequent years, or than Anglo-Welsh ones. They proved to be too cumbersome to administrate and some of the information was dropped after 1855. For this year only, then, one would find all the details given on an English certificate plus:

Parents' ages and birthplaces.
Number of other offspring (alive or already dead) of the
  couple.
Date and place of parents' marriage.

The marriage details were missed out on certificates issued
from 1856 to 1861. Scottish certificates today give all the
details that English ones do, plus the date and place of the
parents' marriage. Copies may be seen at the New Register
House, Edinburgh EH1 3YT.

  In Ireland, civil registration began in 1864, and copies of
entries for the whole of Ireland from that date until 1921 are
with the Registrar General, Joyce House, 8–11, Lombard
Street East, Dublin 2. From 1921 onwards copies of registers
compiled in the Six Counties (Armagh, Antrim, Derry, Down,
Fermanagh and Tyrone) are with the Registrar General for
Northern Ireland, Oxford House, 49–55, Chichester Street,
Belfast BT1 4HL. Irish certificates are similar to English and
Welsh ones.

Adoption

An Adopted Children's Register is kept at the Office of the
General Registrar, Titchfield, Hampshire, although indexes
are at St Catherine's House. These began in 1927; and either
standard or short forms of an adoption certificate can be
obtained from St Catherine's House.

  The General Register Office for Scotland, New Register
House, Edinburgh, has an Adopted Children's Register which
dates from 1930 and is relevant to persons born after October
1909.

6
Marriage

According to the terms of the Book of Common Prayer of Edward VI's reign, marriages were to be performed only between the hours of eight in the morning and twelve noon. However, from an entry dated 10 October 1596 we gather that this was not always adhered to. The parish is St Ebbe's, Oxford, and the entry reads: 'Married Andrew Phipps of Kidlington, and Annis Potter of Kidlington at midnight.' As the compiler of the Oxfordshire Marriage Index remarks, that ceremony would seem to have been either very romantic, or rather sinister!

During the Commonwealth period, civil marriage first came into being under the auspices of an official known as the Lay Register. This gentleman was sworn in before a magistrate, and empowered to marry couples at a cost of 1s.

With the Restoration of 1660, church marriages were again made compulsory, a state of affairs which lasted until 1837 and the re-introduction of civil marriage before a registrar. From 1660 until 1837, therefore, apart from those of Jews or Quakers, the only legal marriages were those performed in the presence of a Church of England clergyman, or another minister belonging to the Anglican Communion, that is to say the Churches of Ireland or Scotland, or the Church in Wales.

Banns and marriage licences

As is still the case today, our ancestors were married either by banns or by licence. Banns were called from the pulpit on three consecutive Sundays. Details may be found either in special Banns Books, in a separate section of the parish register or in the run of marriages. Any typed transcript of a register should also include a mention of banns called for marriages in other parishes, if note were ever made.

A licence cost over double the banns and originated in the

Middle Ages. It allowed a couple to marry without waiting for the three weeks needed for the banns to be read. Reasons for marrying by licence varied: to avoid gossip; to show the more expensive licence was within the couple's means; or in the case of marriages arranged to take place during Lent, or where at least one of the parties was a widow, widower, minor or non-parishioner.

Licences, a rather complex subject, were obtained from several different sources according to circumstances. They could be issued as Special Licences by the Vicar General of Canterbury, in which case they were recorded at Lambeth Palace, or by the Vicar General of York, in which case they can be found at the Borthwick Institute, St Anthony Hall, York. Others were issued by the bishop of the diocese from which at least one of the couple came, by archdeacons, or by the deans of 'Peculiars' (parts of the country which were not under the usual jurisdiction of an archdeacon or bishop). Certain other clergy had Peculiar rights and thus were not answerable to any other authority.

Three documents were involved in the issuing of a marriage licence. The first of these was the Allegation (or affidavit) which was a sworn statement usually by the groom, to the effect that there was no known impediment to the marriage taking place. The main objections were consanguinity or relationship by marriage, an existing marriage, and consent withheld by a minor's parent or guardian. The second document was the marriage bond. This was a security put up as a token of intent that the wedding would indeed take place. Two witnesses, one of whom had to be known to the judge, had to swear that they knew of no impediment. The bond itself was in two parts: the Obligation, a declaration by sureties (one of whom was, once again, normally the groom) stating the sum of money by which they were bound; and the Condition, which stated the names of the couple, and the church, or churches, given as venues for the ceremony.

Only after these procedure had been duly carried out was the licence itself issued. It was taken to the vicar of the chosen parish and the ceremony took place. The officiating clergyman either kept the licence, and stored it with the other parish records, or else it was handed back to the couple themselves.

Very few actual licences still survive, but many indexes have been compiled of them, usually under the archdeaconries concerned; more bonds and Allegations fortunately survive, and they can help to tell us about the licences issued.

Here is an example from the Archdeaconry of Buckingham index:

James Daniel, aged 24, pig-poker,
Ann Toms, aged 32, both of East Claydon.
6th March 1774, at East Claydon.

When dealing with banns and licences, one should bear in mind the fact that they are only expressions of intent to marry; the event did not always take place, as the odd just cause or impediment did arise.

Pregnant Brides

As usual Crabbe has something to say on the subject:

Thus brides again and bridegrooms blithe shall kneel,
By love or law compelled their vows to seal.

The law gave the parish officers the authority to present 'fornicators' whose union proved only too fruitful with a choice between marriage and imprisonment; usually, but not always, the former was decided on.

It seems that the parish, or at least some parishes, may have had a busy time arranging marriages, examinations before magistrates to discover fatherhood, and the punishment of offenders, if the following newspaper extract of 1773 is at all truthful:

The delay of marrying until there is an appearance of an heir would be a great encouragement to matrimony among people in high life.

It has long been the practice of those of the lower class who seldom think of a wedding ring till they are put the alternative: Bridewell or Matrimony, and, one should suppose, this practice might gain some credit at Court for there cannot be a greater economy than in uniting the Christening and Wedding dinner, for, should the parson claim double fees, even he has not a right to a double dinner.

This zeal for chastity, or, failing that, marriage, was some-times the result of economic rather than religious considera-tions; in other words parish officers were just as interested in saving the parish the cost of rearing an illegitimate child and perhaps having to provide for its mother as well, as they were in saving the immortal souls of the wrongdoers.

Those who take an interest in such matters may have noted the discovery, in December 1986, of some seventeenth-century condoms dating from the early years of the Civil War, a hundred years or more before the advent of Mr Condom, if he himself ever really existed. This find was announced on the radio, and an article appeared in no less a newspaper than the *Daily Telegraph* which spoke of the condoms as 'probably the oldest relics of amorous joustings ever found in this country', previous examples having been found from the eighteenth century, but not before.

It seems that the items, five in number, were discovered in 'latrine deposits' by archaelogists working at Dudley Castle, in the English West Midlands, where a Royalist garrison was entrenched for six years. The survival of the condoms was due to the conditions in which they had spent the last 340 or so years and, indeed, they were kept in water for the months during which they awaited laboratory tests. They were analysed, and proved to have been fashioned from fish and animal intestines. They appear, however, to have been designed to protect the wearer from disease rather than his partner from an unwanted pregnancy, and it has been assumed that Cavaliers (or maybe only one inventive Cavalier, due to the fact that only five were found from an occupancy of six years) and camp-followers used them, rather than married couples.

Marriage registers

The marriage entries in the earliest parish registers, the first of which were started in 1538, are often interspersed between the baptism and burial ones although the tidier-minded vicars and parish clerks sometimes divided the events into separate sections. These early entries normally give only the date of the event and the names of the parties, with a place of residence if they lived in a hamlet which formed part of the parish, or if they came from elsewhere. As a rule there are no comments although I recently came across an unexpected one in a tiny Wiltshire parish: 'Married —— bastard, and —— bad whore.' Not a particularly nice item for their descendants to find centuries later.

As mentioned earlier, at one period a lay parish registrar was elected and sworn in before a magistrate, and so, between 1653 and 1658, we have the first instances of civil marriage in this country. The ceremony itself was performed by a Justice of the Peace between the hours of 11 am and 2 pm. As formerly, banns were called three times, although it was no longer necessary to live in the parish. Most of these early civil-marriage records have been lost and, as the registers themselves are frequently deficient during the Civil War and Commonwealth periods, this part of the mid-seventeenth century is a difficult one to research.

Things went on as normal after the Restoration, the next event of national importance being Lord Hardwicke's Marriage Act of 1754, which was designed to put a stop to clandestine weddings (often of minors or heiresses) and to centralise marriage venues. Up until this time ceremonies had taken place in countless little chapels and marriage houses, even in prison, the chief one of which was the Fleet. The obvious example of these 'marriage factories' is, of course, Gretna. The terms of the Act were that a marriage might only be performed after banns had been called three times on payment of the 1s fee, and had been duly recorded in the register-of-banns book, or else a licence had been obtained. The new type of register which came into use from 1755 onwards was a specially printed one with four marriage forms on each page. These forms now included the signatures or marks of the married couple, and those of the clergyman officiating and two witnesses, and stated whether the ceremony was by banns or licence. It also showed whether both the parties came from the parish.

Apart from the bald facts to be obtained from the new registers, there is a little information which one can gain by closer examination of the entries. Do not be unduly alarmed if you find that your ancestor made a mark instead of a signature. This need not necessarily indicate illiteracy, although, of course, it often does mean just that. In any case there was no stigma in being unable to write, particularly if one happened to be a middle-class female of a family where commerce was deemed to be a little vulgar, and one was just not expected to do one's own business. On the other hand, a mark could be a form of politeness if one were in the company of genuine illiterates. It would have been, perhaps, tactless to show off one's writing skills in front of a husband or elderly relative who was not similarly gifted. My own great-grandmother, who was a competent businesswoman and owned stocks and shares in her own name, made her mark on both her marriage certificates; for her own reasons, no doubt. Nor, incidentally, was it a sign of a bad education to spell your name in various ways. After 1755 it can be very exciting to come across one's ancestor's autograph, all shaky with nerves perhaps, but real just the same.

Witnesses, too, can be of interest. Sometimes there may be what amounts to a professional witness who signs at nearly every wedding; he will probably be the parish clerk or a church-warden. More important may be other members of one's family, perhaps not previously encountered. Sometimes there is an indication that a certain ancestor was still alive at the date of his or her offspring's marriage, when you feared, from the individual's disappearance from other sources, that he or she might have already died. Other unknowns may turn out later to be in-laws or members of intermarried families who may oblige with wills or other treasures.

Similarly, mention of other towns and parishes may furnish a vital lead to further registers to be searched. Sometimes these places may be where another branch of the family, or relatives with a different name, came from, or they may, more obscurely, be parishes owned by the same lord of the manor, and with interrelated activities and commerce, although some distance away, even in another county.

When I first started doing my own family-history research, after one or two initial setbacks, I got back to my great-great-great-grandfather James' baptism, as well as finding details of his parents and grandparents in the tiny Oxfordshire village of Spelsbury. What I just could not find, though, was any trace whatsoever of his marriage. I knew his wife's name, Harriet, from baptismal entries for their offspring, and had estimated the date of their marriage to be around the year 1800.

Research into the baptismal registers for parishes lying in ever-increasing circles drawn from Spelsbury yielded nothing.

I checked the 1851 Census, and there was Harriet Ivings, still alive, living at Spelsbury, and described as a 'gloveress'. Her age was given as seventy-five, and her birthplace the neighbouring village of Enstone. Thus, what I then had to do was to check its baptisms for the year 1776 and hope against hope that only one Harriet had been baptised in that year. Having duly obtained the original registers, I started in 1775 – nothing – and then went on to 1776. I worked my way through until December, and then, on the 8th, there she was, Harriet Bryan. I carried on through all of 1777, and was pleased to find no Harriet in sight. So far, so good, but this, of course, was no help at all with the marriage, as they had not been married at Enstone either. I had checked the originals, and the Bishop's Transcripts, and, by this time I had used some two dozen registers from surrounding parishes, and so more or less gave up on them.

Then, suddenly, about two years later, I was looking up an entry for a friend, and, whilst waiting for the register to be brought to me by the CRO staff, I was idly flicking through the Oxford City Marriage Index which had recently made its appearance. I had, by this time, got into the habit of automatically checking anything within sight, whether it looked remotely helpful or not. Imagine my surprise and delight when I came across an entry for 'IVINGS, James, and BRYAN, Harriet, August 3rd, 1801'! The marriage had been celebrated at the city church of St Mary Magdalen, the very one outside which I have stood, month in month out, in all weathers, to catch my bus home after work.

As for the occupations, apart from the isolated mention, these do not come into their own until later. This was in 1813 when, with the passing of George Rose's Act, three separate registers came into being. This at least was the order; some small parishes did not bother to do so until they had used up their current registers.

The more modern registers, then, show local industry with their lists of occupations of the couples and their respective fathers. They also show, incidentally, whether the fathers were still alive at the time of the marriage. There is always an abundance of *agricolae*, which, I am sorry to tell all those who think that they still remember a bit of useful Latin, does not necessarily, in this case, mean farmer but farm-labourer. This mention of jobs helps to distinguish between two individuals with identical names (and, indeed, this is usually the only circumstance in which an occupation is given in the older registers). It can also give some indication of why a newcomer moved into the parish.

The golden rule in writing down entries from a marriage register, and indeed any kind of register, is to write down faithfully every single thing; it may not mean much now but it could prove extremely relevant at a later date, and you may not have the chance to go back and check it again for years. Then, having written it down, sit still at your leisure and actually read and think about what you have found.

An excellent short-cut and alternative to ploughing through all those registers on the off-chance is afforded when a family-history society has been enthusiastic enough to prepare a marriage index. If such a marvellous item exists, all you have to do is to turn to the desired surname, and there they should be, at least a sizeable number of them (the index will have to be incomplete in some ways – as it is such a large undertaking the compilers will have had to stop at a certain date, or exclude some parishes whose registers are not currently available, for example). Even if you do not find the very marriage you want, then at least you should have some idea of which parishes the family frequented in which years.

Helping to compile a marriage index is excellent practice in the ways of family-history research. Apart from it being a socially useful task, you will always have someone to consult about your own research, and you are likely to make friends too. So, if there is not a marriage index in hand for your part of the world . . .

Having said this, it is only fair to point out that not all marriages took place in parish churches, in spite of the fact that only Anglican, Jewish and Quaker marriages were legal until the start of civil registration. Apart from Roman Catholic and Non-conformist marriages, and those of the above mentioned religions and sects, people were also married abroad, by army chaplains, and at sea, and in hospital.

The Public Record Office can offer Non-conformist registers, and those of the Chelsea Hospitals from 1691 to

1765, while St Catherine's House holds Chaplains Abroad registers from 1796 to 1880, regimental registers from 1780 to 1924, and those of Greenwich Hospital from 1724 to 1754. All Roman Catholic registers remain in the parish.

Marriage certificates

English and Welsh marriage certificates, like birth certificates, differ from Scottish ones as regards the information which they contain. They give:

Date and place of the ceremony.

Names of the parties, and their ages (at least as far as 'full age' or 'minor), together with their occupations, marital status and addresses.

Names and occupations of the fathers, and a mention if the father is already deceased.

Signatures (or marks) of the couple and their witnesses.

Marriage certificates are available either from the registrar who registered the wedding (once again if requested before the current register reaches completion only), from the Superintendent Registrar, or from the clergyman, Secretary for Marriages of a synagogue, or Registering Officer of the Society of Friends (Quakers), where the marriage was performed. It is cheaper to obtain a copy of the certificate at the time; the cost is much greater if ordered later. Unfortunately not many of our ancestors had the foresight to provide their descendants with certificates and, as the 'marriage lines' were supposedly kept under the bride's pillow, not that many have survived!

The easiest way, then, of obtaining a marriage certificate, if you live some distance from the place where the ceremony was performed, or if you do not even know where it took place, is to go to St Catherine's House, Kingsway, London, and search the indexes to marriages there. Unfortunately, these listings only give name, date and place, without mention of the spouse, and so, unless you know the names of both parties, there may be some doubt as to which of the several likely people of the name you are looking up is the one which you require. If the spouse's name is known, it is best to look under that surname as well, and thereby cross-check.

Only when you have ordered and received your copy will you be able to see beyond reasonable doubt that you have the correct certificate. If you have, what a find this usually turns out to be, as the family research can not only be pushed back a generation with the establishment of the father of the bride or groom, his occupation and his whereabouts, but you will also be able to add another family, that of the spouse, to those open to research.

Scotland has, as is the case with birth certificates, a specially informative set of certificates for marriages which took place in the year 1855 when civil registration began there. These were also found to be too complicated to administer, and so only for 1855 do we find the following:

Place(s) of current residence.
Details of any former marriages.
Number of children, living or dead.

Current Scottish marriage certificates are the same as English ones, except that they include in addition the name and maiden name of the mothers of the bridal pair. In Scotland marriage may be celebrated in a place of the couple's choosing, not exclusively in an approved building as is the case in England and Wales. It is not uncommon to see a wedding taking place in a hotel or its garden. Scottish certificates are obtainable from the General Register Office for Scotland, New Register House, Edinburgh, as described in Chapter 1.

Irish certificates are similar to English ones, and may be obtained from either the Registrar General, Joyce House, 8–11, Lombard Street East, Dublin 2 (for the Republic and for all Ireland prior to Partition in 1921) or from the Registrar General, Oxford House, 49–55, Chichester Street, Belfast (for those marriages celebrated in the Six Counties after Partition).

Divorce

The year 1857 saw the establishment of a new Divorce Court in London, a measure strongly objected to by the Church. At this time the trial of matrimonial cases was transferred from the ecclesiastical courts to this civil one. In the same year a Divorce Bill came into being, with deep social and religious implications. In 1850 a commission had been set up to enquire into the whole question of divorce, resulting in the 1857 Bill.

Up until this time marriage could be dissolved, but only the wealthy and influential were able to take advantage of this facility. Most people lacked the knowledge of how to set about it and the necessary funds, and indeed the sheer nerve to carry it through. The costs were vast as it was necessary to bring a divorce case first to an ecclesiastical court and then before the House of Lords.

A divorce greatly affected one's standing in society, and so only those with enough cash and panache were likely to attempt remarriage. The lower strata were taught to be content with their lot, and in any case there was the usual fear of a divorced wife becoming a drain on public money; it was bad enough to have to care for families from which the breadwinner had been removed by death. In any case those who had been through the whole rigmarole of applying for a marriage licence should have had long enough to change their minds while they were waiting for it to be issued! Even if he were the guilty party, a husband was still the effective owner of any property which his wife owned, and so there was not much advantage to be had even if a divorce were granted, at least as far as the woman was concerned.

The privilege extended to clergymen by which they may still refuse to marry divorcees in church dates from the events leading up to the setting up of the Divorce Court.

The Act resulting from the Bill did not extend to either Ireland or Scotland. For one thing it was not necessary under the existing Scots law, and for another the Irish did not welcome it as it was contrary to the teaching of the Roman Catholic Church.

A Divorce Register began to be compiled in 1852, before the Act actually came into force, and details of divorce cases are lodged at the Divorce Registry, Somerset House, in the Strand, London.

Lastly, let us consider what most people have only come across in Thomas Hardy's novel, *The Mayor of Casterbridge*, and that is cases where wives were offered for sale. One would suppose that the example which came to Hardy's ears, and which he used in the book, would have been an isolated one, but this excerpt from an article in *Jackson's Oxford Journal* of 1789 makes me uncertain about this:

About noon on Wednesday last, a vulgar mode of Divorce lately adopted, was put in practice here in our New Market Place, before a Multitude of Witnesses.

Richard Hawkins, a Canal Navigator-Man, made a public Sale of his wife to William Gibbs, a Mason employed at the works of the Castle.

After a conversation about the payment of 5/- as the purchase money, the old Husband pulled out a Penny Slip and tied around the Waist of his Wife, the end of which he held fast till he had pocketed three shillings in Part, the Purchaser not abounding in Cash.

He then put the Cord into the Hands of the New Husband and took French leave. The woman immediately called for her second Wedding Ring, which being put on, she eagerly kissed the Fellow with which she walked off, leaving the Spectators in Amazement at such uncommon Assurance.

So, to anyone doing research into either the Gibbs or the Hawkins family tree in Oxford at this period, I can only say 'Good luck!'

Remarriage

A perusal of parish registers and marriage licences will yield a fair number of widows and widowers remarrying, although there are more of the former to be found.

Widows were expected to wait for at least a year before they married again, the theory being that this was the time necessary for the husband's body to return to dust and ashes once more.

Widowers, on the other hand, were encouraged to remarry as soon as they were able to find a suitable mate to care for their motherless brood and, almost certainly, to add to it.

It is not all that common to find widows marrying widowers; when they do, it is generally when they have reached what is politely termed 'mature years'. On the whole, a man usually would choose a younger girl as his second wife, with the hope, no doubt, that she had 'plenty of mileage' in her.

Certain sections of society were completely opposed to widows marrying again under any circumstances. The Victorians, who made quite a cult of death and widowhood, for which they had a splendid example in their Queen, tended to the view that a woman's body belonged to one man alone. She should, they said, remain faithful to his memory until her own demise. Others, anti-cremationists, for example, were worried about what would happen on the Day of Judgement, and how remarried couples would feel when confronted with their original spouses. Needless to say, the average bereaved person was not over-concerned with long-term prospects, but remarried if and when the chance arose, according to the conventions of the age. Some, like Chaucer's Wife of Bath, went through a series of spouses, heedless of the confrontation to come.

7
Work and Play

Before attempting to find out very much about what our ancestors did, and under what conditions, it will almost certainly be necessary to establish where they lived and worked.

One of the best sources for tracing your family, from the late eighteenth century until modern times, is one of the town or county directories. The most comprehensive of these is the Kelly's series, but there are various others including the Post Office Directory and many more local ones. These are to be found in County Record Offices and central libraries. Town directories list streets and their houses, occupants and tenants, while county ones (which sometimes deal with two or more counties together) list the places in the shire, with information on the important attributes, historical and commercial, of each. Most county directories give an account of the local gentry together with the leading members of the community – tradesmen, farmers and craftsmen – and so if great-great-grandfather was a blacksmith or a licensed victualler, a school-teacher or a wheelwright, the odds are he is in one directory or another, just waiting to be discovered.

Occasionally the descriptions of the towns themselves will surprise their present-day residents. How about these three entries from the *Universal British Directory 1790–98?*

WALSALL consists of twelve streets.

CHRISTCHURCH, original name Thunambourn, number of voters 24, pleasantly situated, has a charity school for 24 boys and a large manufactury which employs a number of boys and girls in making watchchains, is famous for a fine salmon-fishery and is thought the first place in England for knit silk stockings.

EGHAM is a large village seated on the Thames, Cooper's Hill has an uniform mass of dullness on which the sun has not bestowed its faintest irradiation.

Censuses

As mentioned in the previous chapters, civil-registration records and the later parish registers can also give some indication of an ancestor's whereabouts and occupation. Further, and more detailed, information about what your ancestor and his or her family did for a living, and what the household consisted of, may be obtained from the Census returns.

Censuses naming individuals, and furnishing details concerning them, have been compiled every ten years since 1841, with the exception of 1941, because of World War II. Those censuses taken prior to 1841 do not provide any information about individuals. The returns are not, as a general rule, made available to the public until 100 years after their compilation; thus the last one to which the public currently has access is the one taken in 1881 for England and Wales.

The returns themselves are kept at the PRO's Chancery Lane building, but microfilm copies for the whole of England and Wales may be consulted at the Search Room, Land Registry Building, Portugal Street, just off Kingsway, London. A move to Chancery Lane is imminent.

It is not always necessary, however, to visit London in order to search the returns as copies are held by many County Record Offices and central libraries for their areas. For a comprehensive guide, see J. S. W. Gibson's *Census returns 1841, 1851, 1861, 1871, 1881, on microfilm: a directory to local holdings* (4th edition 1983). In addition, many family-history societies and local-history groups are busy transcribing and compiling typed transcripts or computer printouts of the returns for individual towns and villages.

Scottish Censuses may be consulted at the New Register House, Edinburgh. These consist of the enumerators' transcript books, which, by the way, are not indexed, but are available to the public up until 1891 (not 1881 as in England or Wales). Irish Censuses are a very hit-and-miss affair, as are

---

Irish Census Return, Dublin, St Kevin's Parade. Note that in Catholic Ireland someone who is not literate in English and not even a Christian, is able to keep himself by giving Hebrew lessons (*Courtesy of the Irish Public Record Office*)

CENSUS OF IRELAND, 1901.

(Two Examples of the mode of filling up this Table are given on the other side.)

FORM A.

No. on Form B. 7

RETURN of the MEMBERS of this FAMILY and their VISITORS, BOARDERS, SERVANTS, &c., who slept or abode in this House on the night of SUNDAY, the 31st of MARCH, 1901.

No.	NAME and SURNAME	RELATION to Head of Family	RELIGIOUS PROFESSION	EDUCATION	AGE (last birthday)		SEX		RANK, PROFESSION, OR OCCUPATION	MARRIAGE	WHERE BORN	IRISH LANGUAGE	If Deaf and Dumb; Dumb only; Blind; Imbecile or Idiot; or Lunatic
					Years	Months	M	F					
1	Mathew Schneider	Head of Fam.	Jew	cannot Read or Write but English	65		M.		Hebrew Teacher	Married	Russia		
2	Hannah Schneider	Wife	Jewess	not English	58			F.		Married	Russia		
3	Elias Schneider	Son	Jew	read & write	24		M.		Dental Mechanic	not married	Russia		
4	Bessie Schneider	Daughter	Jewess	read & write	19			F.		not married	Russia		
5	Leah Schneider	Daughter	Jewess	read & write	15			F.		not married	Russia		
6													
7													
8													
9													
10													
11													
12													
13													
14													
15													

I hereby certify, as required by the Act 63 Vic., cap. 6, s. 6 (1), that the foregoing Return is correct, according to the best of my knowledge and belief.

Thomas McCullagh No. 107 (Signature of Enumerator.)

I believe the foregoing to be a true Return.

Mathew Schneider X (Signature of Head of Family.)

most Irish records; some were intentionally destroyed as soon as they were finished with; some only included certain counties or parts thereof; while yet others were lost during the 1922 fire in Dublin. The survivors are kept at the Four Courts, Dublin 7.

The first and most important requirement, when attempting to use a Census return, is some idea of where the family was living at or near the date on which the Census was taken. At the very least a parish or village is required, and, as previously indicated, these should be obtained beforehand from certificates, directories or family members. It is possible to work one's way through a fair-sized town or city from scratch but this is certainly not to be undertaken if there is any other means of shortening the search.

It is a good idea to arm oneself with a large-scale map of the area showing hamlets and farms. This may help to clarify any difficult writing or damaged parts of the return, and may also suggest neighbouring parishes which just might yield up some information. Towns, by the way, are dealt with parish by parish, and so it is as well to know parish boundaries in built-up as well as in rural areas. Once you give up a microfilm someone else may be waiting to use it, and so do make sure you have explored any likely places before you surrender it.

It is usually simpler to use Census returns locally unless one intends to cover two or more parts of the country, in which case a visit to London is worth while. The drawbacks include the fact that the Search Room at Portugal Street gets very crowded, and you cannot be assured of a microfilm reader as there is no booking system in operation. The ordering system, too, is more complicated than in Record Offices and libraries where a simple form or a verbal request is usually sufficient.

Should a trip to Portugal Street be needed, it is important to arrive as early as you possibly can; failing this come after the peak period of 10.30am to 2.30pm. The Search Room is open to the public from 9.30am until 5.30pm. A reader's ticket to the PRO itself covers entry, otherwise a day pass issued at the door will suffice. Once inside the building you will probably have to queue in order to get a microfilm reader. Do not succumb to the urge to wander off and start looking up what you need in the indexes in advance, because the queue is there so that you can obtain the number of your reader, without which you can do nothing.

Having been allocated a reader, reserve it with some personal belongings, and make sure that you know the correct number. Then you are ready to fill in a request slip. The next step is to find the reference number for the microfilm you need, each complete Census having a separate code. After this, proceed to the indexes, which are colour-coded according to year, and follow the instructions on the board near the index itself in order to look up the place in which you are interested. For large towns street indexes supply exact references for each street, and a list of these towns is available.

Finally, you hand in the completed slip at the requisition counter, and hope that you are not one of the many who are called back to correct some detail or other. Only one request slip is dealt with at a time, and the expected length of time you will have to wait is shown on a board by the counter. Old hands at the game, therefore, plan in advance so that subsequent films are on their way while their immediate predecessor is being consulted.

At last the moment has arrived and you have a film ready to use in your reader, whether you are in London, or at your own local repository. If it is the 1841 Census it will differ from later ones in that it gives only approximate ages, rounded down to the nearest five years. This is an important fact to bear in mind when calculating likely dates for events in an ancestor's life, and why some information concerning age will not tally with that given in subsequent returns. This applies to persons over the age of fifteen, although one occasionally comes across adults entered with their exact ages even in the 1841 return. This Census also gives an occupation. This is often listed as 'NK' (not known), 'FS' (female servant) or 'MS' (male servant). The area of birth is given in the 1841 Census, but not the exact place, merely the county:

Y   Yes, born in county of current residence.
N   No, not born in county of current residence but still born in England and Wales.
I   Born in Ireland.
S   Born in Scotland.
F   Born abroad.

In Censuses from 1851 onwards, the exact age is shown, plus marital status, relationship to the head of the household, exact place of birth and occupation. It is more profitable, therefore, to find one's family in a later Census, but there may still be pitfalls. The enumerators, naturally, were only able to put down what they were told, or what they heard, which was not always correct, particularly in areas where the interviewees spoke a dialect which was unfamiliar. Sometimes deliberate lies were told, usually when the informant was afraid of being sent back to his or her parish of birth and, of course, some genuinely never knew their place or date of birth. One mistake made by the enumerators was to list brothers and sisters of the same surname as a husband and wife; also widowers sometimes turn up as 'unmarried' because they had no wife at the time the Census was taken.

While on the subject of information and pronunciation, if you are as sure as it is humanly possible to be that the family you need is there before your eyes, and yet the required ancestor is missing, look and see if there is another child listed of the same age and sex who could be your quarry in disguise. This is possible with pet names or abbreviations, or short names which could easily be misheard: John for Tom, Will for Bill, Molly for Polly. Obviously the full name should have been given, but it's worth a try; this is how I found my great-grandfather Tom masquerading as a John.

While you have access to a microfilm Census return, do write down every single item of information. That lodger could be a future husband of one of the girls, or a cousin of the family. If at all practical, attempt to write down every mention you can trace of the family and its situation in a Census year. Not only may this prove useful at some future date, but it will serve to give a more complete picture of them in their home district.

That, then, is the Census as an important document in the field of family and social history. With luck one will be able to move back one or two generations by using the details listed under the place-of-birth heading, and therefore locate the appropriate parish registers. Not so immediately important, but also of great interest, are the occupations shown. These could explain why the family moved in the pattern that they did round the country looking for work as, say, shepherds, glovemakers or masons. Apart from the good old British class-consciousness which still lives on in the majority of us to this day, most people are interested in the way in which their forebears earned their living. Were they 'respectable'? Were they paupers or self-employed? Is there any literature likely to be available about their trade or occupation? Is it one that no longer exists outside agricultural shows or craft centres? What was their standard of living?

The most usual jobs listed are 'labourer' (agricultural and otherwise) and 'servant'. Small children are often listed as 'scholars', which sounds very formal when applied to a six-year-old. One does, however, sometimes come up with a rather more unusual occupation, some of which are now difficult for us to decipher. The most misleading is probably the term 'yeoman', as this had slightly different connotations depending on which era it is found in. In the sixteenth and seventeenth centuries, for example, it referred to a man who both owned and worked a smallish estate, a freeholder. He was of a lower status than a gentleman because he actually did some work himself; nonetheless he was of good social standing. In later times a yeoman was taken to mean a countryman, and the distinction of whether or not he owned the land was dropped. Some occupations are obvious, if with a little thought; others are not: a 'mangler' was one who did laundry work and hired herself out to turn mangles; a 'hazler' sold dried flax for linen weaving; a 'bayer' or 'bodger' sold hazel rods for chairmaking or mending; a 'whittawer' was a maker of saddles and horse-collars; and a 'lattoner' was a worker in brass and tin, usually for parts of clocks.

A fairly representative collection of occupations might include (apart from the omnipresent labourers and household staff) scriveners, warreners, soap-boilers, sack-carriers, and, even in Central London, the odd farrier, dairyman and willow-weaver. While on the subject of occupations, how about this advertisement placed in 1757?

WILLIAM DENTON, INSTRUMENT MAKER, ST. CLEMENT'S
Makes Steel Trusses, cures Ruptures, etc.

He likewise makes Steel Collars to prevent Misses hanging down their Heads and also Steel Backs which give young Ladies a Fine shape though they have contracted a bad Habit by uneasy Stays, or any other Accident.

Teeth sent with instructions.

The Denton family, by the way, is still thriving in the varied businesses of selling and hiring out bicycles, selling fruit and vegetables, and running a shellfish stall!

To the modern eye it is amazing how specialised many of the jobs of our ancestors are, and we consider that specialisation is a mark of progress!

Apprenticeship records

As is sadly the case today, there have often been periods in our history when unemployment was a serious problem and youngsters had to take whatever jobs, if any, they could find. The vast majority of children left school well before entering their teens, and many went into service or worked on a nearby estate, went on to the land, or into industry of some kind or another. As was natural, if the father and grandfather had a trade, the son or sometimes daughter was likely to follow in their footsteps, in which case no record is likely to have been made as to their training and conditions of employment.

If the child was to be put to learn a trade under a master who was no relation, he became an official apprentice, and had to have specified terms drawn up regarding his education. Most trades were learned over a specified number of years, only on the completion of which was the apprentice admitted to full membership of his craft or profession.

Apprenticeship records are often known as 'indentures' because they were formed by writing two copies of the document on one sheet, head to head, and then cutting them into halves by means of a wavy or indented line. One copy was kept by the master, and the other by the parent or guardian of the new apprentice.

A stamp duty was introduced on these indentures in 1710, and records of the tax thus payable are to be found in Apprenticeship Books in the Public Record Office for the period 1710–1811. They provide details of the apprentice's name and address, his father or guardian (until 1750) and the name and trade of his master.

Apprenticing an orphan or illegitimate child was a favourite means by which the parish authorities devolved themselves of further responsibility, and so many apprenticeship records are to be found with the other parish records. The Library of the

Society of Genealogists (14 Charterhouse Buildings, London EC1 7BA), contains a large number of copies of apprenticeship records. Others, including originals, are to be found with parish records, family papers, among records of businesses and firms, and even for sale in bookshops.

Notices of apprenticeships to be offered turn up in newspapers, and so it is worth checking your local history collection. Here is an example from *Jackson's Oxford Journal* of 1777:

> Wanted, an apprentice to a Surgeon and Apothecary of good business in Oxfordshire.
>
> A sober, well-conducted lad, who has had a decent Education with a premium of twenty guineas only, provided his parents have no objection to his cleaning boots and shoes and taking care of a horse during his apprenticeship, otherwise a premium of a hundred guineas will be expected.
>
> Enquire of Mr. Bennett, druggist.

Unfortunately not all apprenticeships turned out well and it is not at all uncommon to hear of 'elopements' from a master, as this advertisement, also from Oxford, for the year 1763 shows:

> Eloped from her Master, Mr. Joseph Preaty, Susannah Bedington. She had on when she went a blue and white striped gown, a blue and white Check handkerchief, an old Leghorne Hat and a Pair of Pumps between eighteen and nineteen years of Age and Brown complexioned. If she returns She will be received.

Local newspapers as sources

These are invariably a rich source of family-history material if one is observant and perseveres. Many papers date back to the eighteenth century, some even to the seventeenth. It will doubtless not have escaped notice that many of the examples quoted in this book are taken from *Jackson's Oxford Journal*, Oxford's oldest newspaper, which was started in 1753 by a printer, William Jackson. The Journal survived under the new names of the *Oxford Journal* and the *Oxford Journal Illustrated*, and was then taken over by the *Oxford Times* in

1928. Its name, though, lives on in a weekly paper which is distributed free in Oxford and Oxfordshire to this day. *Jackson's* is by no means the earliest of Britain's newspapers; the *Reading Mercury*, for example, dates from 1723, while others are earlier still, even if complete runs have not always survived.

These early papers were tiny by modern standards, normally about four pages in extent. The reason for this was the stamp duty payable on each sheet. The Stamp Acts were not repealed until 1855, from which date the concise writing so noticeable in previous years tended to grow gradually into full-blown Victorian verbosity. The usual format for pre-1855 newspapers was that the outside pages were devoted to international and national news, while the inner ones were left for reporting local events and for last-minute additions.

We are particularly fortunate in that *Jackson's* has had a wonderful Synopsis compiled in chronological order from 1753 to 1790, and then indexed by person and place; in all, this Synopsis runs to eleven volumes, work on which was started in 1963 by a group of dedicated experts.

It is not exclusively ancient newspapers, though, which prove useful for family-history purposes. Both Mr and Mrs Saunders, whose stories are given in Chapter 3, had very pleasant experiences with English provincial newspapers, Joan's might even be termed atonishing:

During 1982 Bernie had had a breakthrough by writing a letter of inquiry to a newspaper, so, just before Christmas that year, I decided to give it one last fling and write a letter to a Winchester newspaper ... for whatever reason I chose the *Hampshire Chronicle*. Eventually, during February 1983 I received an English letter and I actually said to Bernie, I bet this is from the newspaper saying "sorry, no can do". Well, how wrong I was! It was a letter from a first cousin, the eldest son of my mother's sister, Norah. I could never explain my feelings that day, between laughing and crying; I did not know if I was on my head or my heels.

In the days after, I received more letters from the same family; my aunt had five sons. I also had a letter from another first cousin who was a daughter of one of Mum's brothers. Vera's brother, Keith, would you believe, is a typesetter at the *Hampshire Chronicle* and read my letter to the Editor! My only disappointment was to find out my aunt had died the previous year; she was the last of her family.

Joan goes on to describe a family get-together which her English family arranged in her honour at Winchester:

All my family had contributed in some way to make it a day to be remembered. Relatives came from Liverpool, Southampton, Rickmansworth, and many of the youngsters had never met before. I felt I was walking in my mother's footsteps, sad and wonderful at the same time, to see the church she was married in, the site of her home on the River Itchen, demolished and now a park; to walk along the High Street as she would have done.

Bernie says:

Just to add to Joan's tale, I was the odd man out at the Winchester reunion, being the only person there non-related, except through marriage. It was something to behold! I have never found myself more at home anywhere in my life. I therefore have no hesitation in saying that Winchester was the highpoint of our European tour.

You can imagine the pleasure I experienced when I traced part of my own roots back to there, and I can't wait to trace some living Malkins or off shoots. To me that is what family history is all about. Name-gathering is OK but it is superb to meet the living so that one can see what the genes of the past have given to the present.

What else is there to say apart from get going and write that letter!

The most obvious place to look, in an old newspaper, is under the births, deaths and marriages columns, but do not ignore wedding announcements and coverages of both weddings and funerals. At one time each person present at a funeral was listed, as well as his or her relationship, if any, to the deceased. Also mentioned are representatives of clubs or societies (the British Legion, Mothers' Union, etc) which the deceased belonged to. There are 101 ways in which one can get one's name in the papers; most of them respectable too! So do not scorn the local flower club's annual-show results, the cycling club or the dog trials; you may, by tracing their records, find your white-haired old grandpa as a sprightly twenty-year-old winning prizes galore. You may even come across him, blushing modestly, in some old photograph, as he collects an award of some kind.

While on the subject of newspaper contents, apart from keeping an eye open for any sort of event or competition which your family might have taken part in, do scan the headlines for what was going on at the time. The local papers seem rather more interested in the price of corn than in the Napoleonic Wars, but advertisements, especially those which give price lists, are a fair indication of the cost and standard of living. Our forebears were outspoken in their coverage of the news; something which comes as rather a surprise until one gets used to it. Far from being complimentary about all females in the news ('stunning blonde Miss X' and 'attractive schoolteacher Mrs W.') everyone received a very forthright description, particularly as regards their social status; our ancestors certainly knew their place and everybody else's as well! Last but not least, do have a look at what was considered entertainment, and what was worthy of coverage.

Other sources on work and play

Places of employment and education also keep their own records, perhaps going back hundreds of years in the case of traditional businesses and schools which had their foundation in the Middle Ages or Tudor times. Oxford, Cambridge and Dublin Universities also publish a list of their respective students over several centuries, giving the student's college, place of origin and father's name. Similar publications are available for the Church and the medical world.

On a less exalted level, why not try local and Sunday schools, all of which would have kept a register? Some of the most informative diaries have been written by schoolmasters, doctors and vicars! More recent perhaps, but nevertheless rewarding, can be mill, factory, estate, college and hospital records, not forgetting working men's clubs, the trade unions, and any other organisation where people take out membership or leave some trace of their visits. While being fascinated by our more distant past, too many of us are probably uncertain about where our own parents and grandparents went to school, or at least the exact years that they were there.

Army and navy records

One should consider army or navy papers if an ancestor goes missing for any length of time, or during a period in which the country was at war. The most obvious times are when conscription was compulsory, but ancestors 'took the King's shilling' on and off throughout the last three centuries, even if they only got as far as joining the local militia.

The Public Record Office holds army lists, giving details of officers, commissions and regiments from 1754 onwards. It also has Casualty Returns for the years 1809 to 1857, which list a man's rank, trade, next-of-kin and birthplace, and give a copy of his will if available. The Chelsea Hospital baptisms (1691–1812), marriages (1691–1765) and burials (1692–1856) are also held at the PRO. Other more specialised army records held there include details of courts martial 1684–1847, Description Books from 1756, Militia Returns (which were compiled by the Lord Lieutenant of each shire for the Quarter Session records, and mention officers, non-commissioned officers and men from 1769), muster-rolls from 1708 for each regiment (from 1795 some give the place of birth, and age on enlisting), and lastly, pensions. Lists of veterans discharged from regiments also make interesting reading. Here is an entry for a soldier discharged from the 66th Wiltshire Foot: 'James Cooper admitted 1820, aged 35. Served 26 years including two under age. Complaint: supernumary and worn out. Born Troubridge, weaver, height 5'7¾", dark brown hair, hazel eyes, dark complexion.' It must have been quite depressing to have given most of your life, from age nine, and then to be dismissed as 'supernumary and worn out'.

Navy records, too, are mostly in the care of the Public Record Office. These include Bounty Papers of payments to seamen and their families from 1685 to 1822; Description Books, giving brief physical details, age and birthplace, from 1790 onwards; records of the apprenticeship of children of pensioners at Greenwich Hospital; entry and discharge details of these pensioners themselves from 1704 to 1869; muster-rolls of ships' companies giving name, rank, age and birthplace, from 1680 but complete only from 1740 onwards; lists of names and commissions of officers from 1749; pay books from 1669; and pension books from 1734 to 1885.

When the latter concern widows, the marriage certificates should be attached where they existed.

Photographs and postcards

Of course, our ancestors did not spend every waking minute at work, although, to many of them, it probably seemed as if this were the case. The Victorians and Edwardians were great writers of letters, diaries and postcards, many of which survive. They also seem to have taken a vast amount of photographs if the number of survivors is anything to go by. Unhappily, the great majority of those photographed are condemned to oblivion because there is no-one left alive who can identify them. A major source of photographs and postcards, apart from the family album, of course, may be the overseas branch of the family, one more reason to write to those Australians or Canadians. Cards were often made from portrait photographs, and sent off to distant relatives in ways which would seem quite immodest to us. It is quite usual to see a photo of Aunt Elsie simpering away in a cardboard folder with a robin on the front and Season's Greetings inside. Needless to say, most of these were sent away rather than being kept by the sitter, and so there can be half a dozen or so copies lying around unsuspected in loft or cellars.

School photographs usually raise a smile. See if the school itself still has a copy. If it does, maybe the photographer is still in business and can provide one for you.

Even if you are not lucky enough to have in your possession postcards which relate to your actual family, they can, nevertheless, furnish considerable information if local postcard fairs are searched. Most dealers display their wares under counties, and so it is an easy task to flick through to see if you can come up with a card of the ancestral town or village in grandfather's day. With perserverance you may even find one with the family business or dwelling on it, but even if there is nothing personal about it, it will still serve as a piece of social history which was around at the same time and in the same place as your ancestor. The great thing about local-view postcards is that they can be dated fairly accurately and that the scene they depict is invariably labelled. Even if there is no date stamp, in the case of an unused card for instance, an expert, or local historian will not have too much trouble dating it, within a year or two, by studying the fashions, transport, shop-fronts and similar clues. A word of caution is called for as regards fashions, though, both in postcards and in photographs: bear in mind that local finery was likely to be way behind that of London, or even the county town, and that 'photo' dresses might only see the light of day on high-days and holidays.

The sending and reproducing of postcards and identified photos can be a two-way process between branches of the family. Nowadays it is possible to obtain high-quality copies of either for a matter of pence. Copies should always be used instead of the real thing if it is necessary to handle them or send them through the post.

Then we come to the reverse side of postcards. Sometimes the message is more rewarding than the view itself, especially if it happens to be a card from the family collection. If you are lucky there may be some item of news, a birth or death, a family holiday or a new member by marriage. Look out for changes of name and address. Less exciting, but still interesting, are the little peeps we are given into everyday life: spelling, dialect expressions, the way people addressed each other ('My Dear Brother'), the speed and efficiency of the postal service, weather, seasonal pursuits; the list is endless. A friend of mine has the postcard collection belonging to a young girl who lived in a village at the foot of the Berkshire Downs at the beginning of this century. By means of the cards one can, as one works through the album, watch her grow up from a little child, through adolescence until she meets her 'young man'. To start off with she is Miss Orpwood to him, then Bessie and 'my dearest girl', until the name changes from her maiden name to his. He goes to France, sends her several patriotic cards, then returns safe and well as far as we can make out. The last of the early cards are signed 'from your hubby' as the couple settle down to married life. At the far end of the album is a new run of more modern cards, mainly birthdays and Christmas, to 'Our Dear Mum and Dad', until finally Bessie and her Bert become 'Nannie and Grampa' on the cards from the seaside. Quite a little family history in its own right!

Even if you are not able to find anything in the postcard line of sufficient local or personal interest to buy, it is worth going into the local-history collection of your library where they are

125

sure to have their own collection of photographs and postcards, which will probably date from last century and may well prove of interest. Some libraries produce copies for a few pence each. If you have any treasures of your own, they will be able to date them approximately, and even identify features in them.

Quarter Session records

These records, which are now generally held by County Record Offices, were compiled from Tudor times until the 1970s. They finish at that time because this was when a Local Government Act transferred the bulk of the Quarter Sessions' non-judicial responsibilities to the newly-formed County Councils. Quarter Session records, as the name suggests, deal with the outcome of the meetings of the Justices of the Peace who convened four times a year at Easter, midsummer, Michaelmas and the Epiphany. The records were kept by the Clerk of the Peace, a professional lawyer. Originally they were stored in the form of rolls, hence their alternative name, Quarter Session Rolls. By now a large number have been copied, catalogued and indexed.

These records deal with practically every aspect of human life and behaviour: religion, taxes, licences, the poor and insane, theft and burglary, public and private morals, defence, brewing, any highway and byways. They are not merely lists of offenders, but also tell us about which members of the community were parish officers and county officials, applied for game or public-house licences, or brought actions against each other. They are sometimes a help with cases of illegitimacy as the father's name may come to light during appearances before a magistrate, but not be written elsewhere.

Similar to Quarter Session records are City Archives, which also feature the most ordinary of ancestors. Here is an entry for Hereford, 1691, in which a local butcher is being fined for insanitary behaviour: 'We present John Blunt, butcher, for keeping a misken [midden] and emptying his garbage or beasts' bellies in the open street leading from Fryers Gate to St Nicholas' Church. Pained 3/4d every week if not cleaned once a week.'

Trial records of any type are always interesting. Even those who are afraid of discovering the proverbial skeleton in the cupboard (or in the closet if the skeleton happens to be an American one) may find that the black sheep was guilty of little more than poaching, receiving stolen goods or helping himself to a loaf of bread. Retribution was swift and harsh, and capital offences were numerous.

Here is an extract from a letter which was intercepted shortly before the trial of a certain Miles Ward who, in March 1784, was accused of stealing a quantity of altar plate from Magdalen College Chapel, Oxford. This letter is written in a form of thieves' cant known as 'St Giles' Greek', which was spoken in the notorious St Giles High Street area, just off London's Charing Cross Road. Ward is writing to a former partner in crime, William Cox, now turned informer:

> I don't blame thee for turning Stag [informing against me] for, to be sure, every man has a right to take care of his own self, but what made thee tell so many lies to the Queer Cuffin [the magistrate]?
> How coudst say that the Golden Stick [candlestick] at New College Chapel is stuck all with Diamond and that there was a design to nab [steal] it and make all our Fortune, when everybody knows that it is but a thin, hollow thing, with bits of blue glass, not altogether worth ten pounds?
> Thou hast the luck to squeak [inform] now, and so thy friends must go to quod and scour the Crampings [go to prison and polish fetters with their ankles].

The outcome of the trial was that Ward was found guilty, and executed on 27 March 1784. His body was put into a 'handsome coffin and carried away by his mother to Walham Green in a smuggler's Caravan and Pair which she had ordered down to Oxford for that Purpose'.

Poll Books

These lists of who voted at parlimentary elections, and how their votes were cast, are so called because 'poll' is an old word for head, and thus they consist of a 'head count' of all those entitled to vote. They therefore constitute a fairly full list of the property-owning classes in the late eighteenth and the nineteenth centuries. Apart from the name, and the way the person voted, Poll Books usually state where he lived, and where the property was that entitled him to vote.

Apart from the obvious interest to anyone researching their

ancestors in their own county, Poll Books, like indexes of any kind, help by showing places where a certain name was to be found at a given time, and so are useful to anyone working in a strange county.

The practice of knowing, and indeed publishing, how a man voted seems rather shocking to those of us brought up to respect the system of the secret ballot. The following newspaper item, though, makes it clear that only too often voting was less than democratic, and the outcome more or less a foregone conclusion. This report appeared in 1753, again in *Jackson's*, and it refers to the forthcoming election of 1754, an important one in Oxfordshire as it was a controversial struggle between radicals on one side and reactionaries on the other, as represented by Sir James Dashwood and Lord Harcourt, of Kirtlington and Bampton respectively.

A Receipt to make a Vote: by the Cook of Sir J. D. . . . . . . d.
Take a cottager of thirty shillings a year – tax him at forty – swear at him – bully him – take your business from him – give him your business again – make him drunk – shake him by the hand – kiss his wife – and he is an honest fellow.
    N.B. The above cook will make an affidavit before any Justice of the Peace that this receipt has been try'd on the body of Billy S . . . . fe and several others in the neighbourhood of K . rtle . . n and never fail'd of success.

A Receipt to make a Majority of Votes at the next Election by L . . d H . . . . . . t's Cook.
Take all your lifehold tenants and make them freeholders, tax them as such immediately, and, less the election should come on before they are legally qualified, antedate their leases, this, with a little calve's head soop [*sic*] will effectually answer the purpose.
    N.B. It has been tried on many in the Hundred of B . .pt . n.

Hearth Tax returns
The Hearth Tax was levied between the years 1662 and 1689 at a rate of 2s for each hearth which a household possessed. Those who received Poor Relief, or whose houses were valued at less than 20s per annum and who were not paying parish rates were not made to pay the tax. Householders were listed by the Parish Constable, their hearths numbered against their names, and the lists forwarded to the Justice of the Peace at the Quarter Sessions. The tax itself was collected twice a year, at

Michaelmas, and on Lady Day (25 March).

Some returns have been printed or published by local-history societies.

Miscellaneous records

Every library and Record Office will have documents which are peculiar to its own district. These may include maps, surveys, photographs, diaries, registers, wages, books and estate papers, memoirs, and items of more or less exclusively local interest on such topics as folklore, customs or ghosts, for example. Each repository is different, and its stock will be added to constantly, so do make the best possible use of what it has to offer, and perhaps save yourself a trip further afield by asking the staff's advice on whatever interests you.

Manorial records

Lastly we come to what is probably the most fascinating and, at the same time, the most difficult and frustrating of all family-history sources, the manorial records. Do not be misled into thinking that manors faded out of existence centuries ago; they and their influence lived on well into the last century; indeed some still survive today in an altered form. Lords of the manor were a very varied set of people, some of them bishops or archbishops.

Manorial records can cover a vast range of topics, but the ones of most value to family historians are Court Rolls and Court Books, Rent Rolls, and Relief Rolls (also known as Quit Rents).

Manor Courts were held, and what went on was written down first in Court Rolls, and at a later period in Court Books. Until 1732 the records were kept in Latin, apart from a lapse into English during the Commonwealth period, after which they resumed in Latin once more. The format in which the proceedings were noted varied little over the centuries, whichever language was being used, and so it is as well first to examine a nineteeth-century Court Book, which will be in a fair handwriting as well as in English, so that you may accustom yourself to the procedure involved.

The value of Court Books and Rolls to family historians lies in the fact that, sooner or later, most people could be reasonably sure of appearing in them, so comprehensive was their scope. They list those present at the court itself, with apologies for absence and fines for those without good reason for staying away. Surrenders of land are noted, together with the details of those entering into it. The main business of the day is followed by the conclusions that the court arrived at. When you know your way through the agenda, so to speak, you will know which bits to concentrate on and which you may safely skip.

If you are really lucky, you may come across a helpful passage in which one or two generations of your family can be identified from each other, as sons succeed fathers, and younger brothers older ones. Not only can you find out who was the father of whom, but you can also discover where in the parish they lived, in what sort of accommodation, and what they paid to rent it. If the amount which they paid was minute, even judged by the standard of what everybody else on the manor was paying, this may be an indication that other, more valuable land or property was being rented elsewhere. Sometimes even a forthcoming marriage may be mentioned at the court, when a young couple presented themselves in order to ask permission to rent land and property from the manor after their marriage. This should lead to a close perusal of the parish registers and, we hope, the discovery of a wedding.

Rent Rolls, which are lists of rents collected, do not give any information about the people they are concerned with, though, like Court Books or Rolls, they may prove invaluable as regards proving relationships. This is particularly true of the seventeenth century, when so many parish registers are defective towards the middle of the century as a result of the civil wars and religious quarrels. They also prove that an ancestor was alive and in the parish, or at least on the manor, at a given time. Incidentally, parishes are not always synonymous with the manors as there may have been more than one parish covered by the land belonging to a manor; similarly land from more than one manor may have come under one parish.

Relief Rolls (perhaps more safely known as Quit Rents because of the confusion which can so easily arise between the first name and lists of people receiving parish relief) constitute a sort of cross between Rent Rolls and Court Books; so, if one type of record is missing or illegible, there is always the chance that another may provide a clue. The 'relief' involves one tenant giving up his land or property, and another relieving him of the lease. Thus these rolls give information very similar to that recorded in Court Books, but without all the other details to work your way through.

Manorial records sometimes show the relationships between places as well as between individuals. Villages which appear to have no connection with each other, and are situated at some sizeable distance away from each other, sometimes belonged to the same Lord of the Manor, and a link was forged between them both economically and socially. This can sometimes explain why someone travelled halfway across the next county to set up in business, or why he married a girl from a distant parish. When a young man had finished his apprenticeship within the family business to become a wheelwright, say, or a smith, he might be surplus to the needs of his own village, and so the Lord of the Manor might set him up elsewhere on another part of his land where such a craft was needed.

Manorial records are usually kept by County Record Offices, although this is by no means always the case. If you suspect that somewhere in which you are interested may have had more manorial records than the CRO can offer, and the CRO cannot tell you of their whereabouts, one option is to write to the Royal Commission on Historical Manuscripts (Quality House, Quality Court, Chancery Lane, London WC2A 1HP), which will tell you whether the documents do in fact exist, and where they are to be found. An enquiry about several small Oxfordshire manors yielded the information that, far from being safely gathered at the Oxfordshire County Record Office, they were spread as far afield as Exeter Cathedral Library, Arundel Castle Library, the Public Record Office and Gloucestershire County Record Office.

These important, valuable and captivating documents, even when traced, may not give up their secrets without a struggle. They may be in a bad state of repair, be written in dog Latin with a blunt quill and cheap ink, or, however beautiful, be simply too complex for the amateur to decipher. The important point is that they have survived at all, and sooner or later someone will be able to transcribe them for you if you try hard enough, and, of course, are willing to pay for the service.

8
Parish Life

Although the Church had been organised into parishes for hundreds of years, the parish did not really come into its own as a social and economic as well as a religious unit until after the Reformation, a process that had already been hastened on its way, however, by the Wars of the Roses and the breakdown of the feudal system.

One might well be forgiven for thinking that the Reformation was achieved by Henry VIII single-handed, with the sole object of marrying Anne Boleyn and divorcing Katherine of Aragon. The Act of Supremacy of 1534, by which Henry broke the hold of the Roman Catholic Church on England and Wales, was, in fact, preceded by a series of religious reformers, the most recent and forceful of whom was Martin Luther earlier in the sixteenth century.

The importance of the English Reformation was the fact that Henry, by making himself the head of the new Church of England, had managed to superimpose the authority of the monarch on the nation, in place of that of the Pope in far-off Rome. The new state religion, Protestantism, declared that each man was responsible before God for his own good or evil acts; no longer was the prospect of Heaven to be brought nearer by the purchase of pardons and indulgences. From this reign on, then, we hear increasingly of the religious convictions of the individual man and woman of the field and in the street, rather than only of those clerks in holy orders.

Once the break was made with Rome, and Catholic beliefs had been challenged, the floodgates were open for the views of various groups of dissenters. First came the Protestants themselves, a blanket term for all who refused to acknowledge the authority of the Pope, then the Puritans, then the dozens of larger and smaller sects which appeared in the seventeenth century. We moderns may well find it almost impossible to understand what all this furore over religion was about, and how it could be worth the bloodshed, imprisonment, torture and burnings.

How did the break with Rome affect the everyday life of the nation? What has all this to do with family history? The answers are complicated, political and economic as well as religious, and would merit a book to themselves, but the crux of the matter is the way in which society reorganised itself after this social and religious upheaval, and, above all, how it coped with the very real problem of dealing with the poor.

The Poor Law

At the Dissolution of the Monasteries, which took place between 1536 and 1539, some 616 religious houses were suppressed, thus adding, according to some estimates, 15,000 or so people to the existing high numbers of unemployed persons. Naturally the majority of these were monks, nuns and others in religious orders, but to these must also be added those employed in a lay capacity by the great monasteries and institutions; the household, farm and estate workers, for example. Also, the religious bodies had made themselves responsible for a large number of the needy, sick and dying who had nowhere else to go. So, at one stroke, a type of career, a source of employment, and a social service were destroyed.

Late Tudor times saw the problem of beggars and vagrants, on a scale which had not been apparent since the breakdown of society during the Black Death and the ensuing Peasants' Revolt in the mid and late fourteenth century. The first attempts at dealing with the nuisance was a policy of whipping, branding and similar punishments for homelessness and poverty, but by 1562–3 in Elizabeth's reign an Act had been passed to compel parishes to make assessments of the needs of the parochial poor, and to levy a Poor Rate accordingly. It is the workings of this Poor Rate which generated much of the body of parish records which are so valuable to family historians today. The first Act to follow was that of 1601, which served as the foundation for the whole code of practice which was in use for centuries afterwards.

Subsequent Acts, notably those of 1662, under Charles II, and of 1697, in the reign of William III, defined most strictly the terms by which a person was entitled to residency, and

Brot forward — £48 16 11
Genuiey 9 Paid for Meating —
and sheurting for the workhouse 3 11 4
Genuey 12 Paid Huntlow Sheep Bill
for the workhouse — 0 8 11½
12 Paid William Gilkins his Bill — 13 3½
12 Paid for Clothing for the workhouse 1 4 1
spent at Chalbey — 0 4 0
Paid John Study for Goin to
Bramson for shough Good — 0 8 0
and for shough — 0 6 0
and spent the same time — 0 7 2
Genuey 15 Pd Wellison 4 new Peard of
coulting shues for the workhouse — 1 15 4
Genuey 21 Paid Mr Gvins his Bill — 0 0 6
for Bred for the workhouse 4 15 6
Genuey 25 Pd Mr Phillips for the 0 0 0
Bred for the workhouse 11 11 0
Genuey 26 Pd Edward Huntlow 0 0 0
for heall when the workhouse
wase set and when the good 0 0 0
wase lookover and for the
drink for the workhouse — 1 11 0
Febey 1 Paid Spandel for 1 meinh
the 8 Copres for the workhouse 0 5 6
Febey 3 Paid the Builuesso mate 0 7 7
Febey 6 gave shough wife 0 0 0
for Bry some linen 1 5 6
Febey 14 Paid for close for the
workhouse — 1 5 4
spent the same time — 0 1 6
March 9 Paid William cutting for
the shues and Making shifts — . .
for soap for Thds — 1 12 11
December 7 Paid Washbon — 0 1 0
£82 10 7

18 73 Ann Hook
December 20 Pd 1 wick Hize
Pd Chales Farmer 1 wick
Pd Thomas Feld 1 wick
Pd William Bowel 1 wick
Pd Ann French 1 wick
Dec 21 Pd painting
Pd John suche 1 wick
Pd samuell Gvins 1 wick
Pd Thomas Griffin 1 wick
Pd Mary Gvins 1 wick
Pd William Molding 1 wick
Pd Thomas Griffin
Pd samuell Bowel 1 w
Pd Night 1 wick
Pd John suche 1 wick
Pd Gorge Mayo 1 wick
Pd Betey Wilkins 1 wick
Dec 22 Pd for Meat for the Wor
Pd Tennant Child 1 w
Pd Jmme Maigets 1 wick
Pd Eliz Bowel 1 wick
Pd Eliz Chirnell 1 wick
Pd Ann suche 1 wick
Pd Fancy Rainbow 1 w
Pd Eliz Ffenches 1 wick
Pd Eliz Beeding 1 wick
Dec 22 Pd Eliz and sedah Jour
Pd the Svows-hyed 1 wick
Pd Mary Forkner 1 wick
Dec 26 Pd Mary Givnes

thereby to benefit from the parish. Although there were additions and alterations, the basic terms of these Poor Law Acts and Acts of Settlement stated that in order to claim from a parish one must fulfil one of the following conditions:

1. Have been born there, or one's father must have been born there.
2. If under 7 and legitimate, one's father must live there.
3. Marry a parishioner.
4. Work there for one year if single, or childless.
5. Take up apprenticeship, in which case employers were sometimes asked to put up a sum of money in order to recompense the parish if the need arose.
6. Rent property worth £10 or more per annum.
7. Hold public office.
8. Pay the parish rate, ie contribute to the poor oneself.
9. Be resident in the parish for forty days, having already given prior notice in writing to the parish authorities. One could be forcibly removed if it were shown that one was likely to become a liability, even if one had not actually done so.
10. Put up a sum of money as a sort of bond of good faith and ability to pay.

These Acts, far from solving the problem of the poor, led to great harshness in their administration, and also to a certain amount of abuse. Some parishes became almost depopulated as the richer sections of society attempted to keep out all but persons of independent means. The more wealthy also had a tendency to raise objections to the marriage of poor people in case their future dependants became those of the parish as well. Moreover, some unscrupulous employers would hire servants only to discharge them again before the qualification period of a year was up. Unemployment was much more severe in some parts of the country than others and, even if there were jobs to be filled, workers were not free to roam the country looking for employment. Unless one were a

Overseers of the Poor Account, late eighteenth century, from north west Oxfordshire and showing individual interpretation of the local dialect, not to mention eccentricities of spelling! (*Courtesy of Oxfordshire County Record Office*)

craftsman, confident of specific work in one particular place, for example a mason commissioned to work on a stately home, or a Cambridge college, there was little mobility to search for work elsewhere, and the poor were more or less bound to their native parishes.

The Settlement Act of 1697 forbade strangers to take up residence in a parish without a Settlement Certificate to prove that their own parish would accept them back again should they ever be in need of relief. This was particularly relevant in the case of seasonal workers, and those doing temporary work of any kind such as helping with harvesting.

If no certificate was forthcoming, the new parish could issue a document known as a Removal Certificate, which was the result of referral to the Justices at the Quarter Sessions, in the case of a dispute between two parishes. Both Settlement and Removal Certificates should be with the County Record Office, or the rest of the parish records if still in the parish.

A parish's attitude to outsiders seems very hostile to us today, although similar instances occur in our own times with regard to immigrants, whom some wish to see removed to their supposed countries of origin, regardless of the human suffering involved. In our ancestors' day, however, everyone was more directly involved, certainly those from whose pockets the money was actually coming. An officer known as the Overseer of the Poor was appointed by the Justice of the Peace, and he was responsible for the collection and distribution of the money involved. You will remember that the Act of Elizabeth's reign had forced a levy on those able to pay. This meant that they had to be assessed, and their contributions noted and duly collected. The rest of the money given to the poor was made up of donations and legacies from various charities, although, of course, such things were by no means always forthcoming in every parish.

The Overseer of the Poor, then, was in a rather unenviable position. On one hand he was liable to be pestered by both the genuinely destitute and those who thought they might give it a try, for scroungers, like the poor, are always with us. No doubt some of the cases really were tragic and touched his heart, but, on the other side, he was responsible for the sensible disposal of the cash and goods and, as such, was answerable to the more influential members of the parish, in other words the contributors.

Not only were the poor to be helped; orphans had to be arranged for, and the pauper dead to be buried. Sometimes, the time of the Civil War being a good example, soldiers died in the parish without even leaving their names, let alone enough money for a funeral. The same applied to gypsies and other travellers; it was all very difficult.

Things had got to such a state in eighteenth-century Oxford that:

> ... [the] Justices passed a resolution at Quarter Sessions not to grant passes in future to any Vagabond without ordering that they shall be whipped from County to County. This Resolution had been found necessary in many other Counties as the whole Kingdom has been burthened with the expenses of these Vagabonds as the cost alone of sending them to their own Parishes, which, according to Act of Parliament, is done at the 'trifling cost' of sixpence a mile.
> (*Jackson's Oxford Journal*, April 1767)

In larger towns it was not unknown to hear of the emaciated corpses of those who had died of hunger being found. Dr Johnson reported that he had heard that some twenty people a week died in London of malnutrition. The town centres in industrial areas were overpopulated slums, but rural districts were not always much of an improvement, especially in the case of absentee landlords or semi-deserted villages.

Parish administration

Let us return to our typical parish, where the Overseer is still doing his best for his charges, and the other members of the parish council will be keeping accounts of their administrative duties.

The Vestry, for example, so named after that part of the church where it originally met but long since transferred to the Black Bull next door, keeps a Minute Book. The Vestry is composed of church members and is an early type of local government. Some Vestries are 'open' ones to which any parishioner may come, while others are 'closed' and exclude all but the leaders of the community.

The Minutes incorporate a list of the parish officers each

year, including the Overseer, of course, the churchwardens
and the Inspector of Highways too. Also listed are 'Briefs', ie
collections made for various worthwhile causes and charities.
These are sometimes longstanding, but are more frequently for
disasters such as a burned-down church, or flood victims.
They relate not only to this county, or even to this country, but
sometimes include help sent to Christian communities
overseas. Vestry Minutes are sometimes to be found in the
parish registers themselves; others are in separate Vestry
Books.

Other products of parish administration include Poor Rate
Books, which are the actual lists of assessments of those liable
to pay contributions towards the upkeep of the poor. This is a
forerunner of our rates system, except that it is based on the
rateable value of the *person* and not of the property
exclusively. Care should be taken not to confuse Poor Rate
entries with the listings of who was receiving (as opposed to
giving) what.

Very informative, and often humorous, are the
Churchwardens' Account Books. Churchwardens, usually
two in number, but sometimes as many as four, were leading
members of the parish. Their duties were varied and included
the care of church property and its income; the upkeep of the
parish registers, under the supervision of the incumbent,
naturally; the supervision of the Poor Relief; the ensuring of
regular attendance at church; the presenting of offenders at
church courts; arranging baptisms and burials of strangers left
in the parish; and all the miscellaneous workings of the
Church, material and spiritual.

Their accounts present a full picture of parish life, in some
instances from the Middle Ages onwards, certainly from the
eighteenth century. These gentlemen were not always the best
of spellers, as one suspected from their attentions to the parish
registers. When they are given their heads in the accounts, the
effect is sometimes rather startling. The entries for people who
were receiving payment described as one or two 'wicks'
puzzled me for a minute in one tiny parish. Fortunately I soon

Churchwardens' Accounts, South Newington, Oxon, 1617. Note the first
writer's showy penmanship, followed by varyingly successful attempts on
the part of the Churchwardens. (*Courtesy of the Vicar, Rev Dr Edward
Condry*)

Whereas heretofore yt hath beene accustomed
tyme out of mynd, to gather for the maintenance of
the Clarke yearelye, sixteene pence for every
yard land,. Therefore wee whose inhabitante
of the towne of South Molton have nowe agreed
that the said sixteene pence for a yard land shall
Continue to bee paid yearely as aforesaid on
the first day of may, for the maintenance if the
Clarke as aforesaid for ever, In witnes
whereof wee have hereunto sett oure
hande the sixth of Maye Anno Dni 1617

Phillip Boxe

William D (marke) Smith

William (marke) Tynne

William (marke) Dampion

Thomas TR (marke) Roberts

Robart Frend

Francis (marke) Browne

Peter T (marke) Tonnatt

William Roobe

William Gyles

John I (marke) Clifford

realised that they were being paid by the 'week' and not being given candles.

The cost of living, and indeed of wages, is fully represented in the accounts. I have before me photocopies of Churchwardens' Accounts dating from the 1770s:

		Brot forward	£	s	d
Genery 9	Paid for sheeting and shurting for the workhouse		3	11	8
Genury 19	Pd William Coulling 4 nue Peire of Shues for the workhouse		1	15	6
Genury 21	Paid Mr. Evins his Bill for Bred for the workhouse		0	0	0
			7	15	6
Genury 26	Pd Edward Hunslow for heall [ale] when the workhouse wase set and when the Goods wase Lookover and for the Drink for the Workhouse		1	11	0
Febery 3	Paid the Bucher for mate			7	7

In this case, the parish is Spelsbury, Oxfordshire, the writing is immaculate, which in a way makes the spelling even more obvious, and the payments are kept in a separate book from the dole proper. The way in which the churchwarden has interpreted the pronunciation, and set down the local version, is interesting because many of the words are still so pronounced by the older generation in west Oxfordshire. It would be a pleasure to compile a social and economic history of the times nearly exclusively from such accounts.

Churchwardens' Accounts are not always devoted exclusively to payments made to, and on behalf of, parishioners. In this conservation-conscious age it is disturbing to find this set of payments (made on 17 April 1773) in the accounts of Holywell (otherwise known as St Cross) Parish, right in the heart of the City and University of Oxford:

To cash for destroying 52 hedgehogs	£0 17s 0d.
To cash for 9 polecats	£0 6s 0d.
To cash for 49 doz. sparrows at 2d. per doz.	£0 8s 2d.

What value can one expect to be put on the life of a sparrow or a hedgehog, though, when the quality of human life counted for so little?

How then, did our ancestors manage to deal with the ever-present problem of coping with the high rate of unemployment, and how successful were they? Family historians, at least when they begin, are often a little shocked to discover their family living 'on the parish'. This was certainly nothing to be ashamed of; it happened even in well-run families, for, if there was no work to be found, how could anyone be expected to be self-supporting without independent means? The number of poor was a reflection of the economic situation rather than indicating any fecklessness on the part of the breadwinner.

The able-bodied poor were, in theory, the responsibility of the parish as it was supposed to find them work. This was indeed the case where road-building, or maintenance was needed from time to time, but obviously this hit-and-miss method was not able to provide for everybody all year round. Most of the population involved was not fit for anything apart from general labouring; it was not as if they were even fully literate, at least if the couple making the following declaration (dated 23 January 1773) were anything to go by:

I, Josseph and Eslebtah Weller by Ockepachant a Tayler in Blechinton dou ombeley icknoeleg that we bowth did abuss and scandliss Mrs. Price at the Green Man in the sam Parish and thiss by the Order of Jestess provis that all we sed wass falss.

In any case, many people in the parish would not have been able to work even if there had been anything for them to do. As regards the aged, and the sick, for example, some parishes paid for their rent and food, while others boarded them out. Some had set up workhouses, under the terms of an Act of 1723, and, after Gilbert's Act of 1782, they were allowed to combine with other parishes in order to make a Union and thus found a joint workhouse for which all the parishes concerned were responsible. Thus, when you are reading through an old directory, you will be told to which Union a certain parish belonged, usually named after the leading parish.

Babies usually had rather a rough deal in cities, where they were only too frequently abandoned or their corpses dumped.

Disease and illegitimacy were rife, and in any case the parents were probably unknown. Orphans, therefore, were a great problem for parish officers. Some were put into the workhouse, while others were put out to nurses for a small fee. These often died of neglect. Children could be apprenticed from the age of seven until they reached twenty, in order to learn a trade, and this method relieved the parish of the cost of their upbringing. Sometimes they were sent to another parish to take up their apprenticeship, where, if they lasted the necessary forty days, they became entitled to settlement rights. Children ran the danger of becoming little better than slaves, and many 'eloped' from their masters, as we have already seen. Even if this happened, the master was still entitled to a £5 fee from the parish, and it was possible for unscrupulous employers to take on a child, ill-treat or overwork him or her until the child ran away, and then apply for another one, perhaps to another parish.

The estimated cost of keeping the poor at the beginning of the last century was £4 million pounds in 1803, doubling to £8 million by 1818, the increase being the result, no doubt, of the Napoleonic Wars, which had broken out in the meantime, and left many a family fatherless. By 1832, however, the cost had dropped to around £6½ million, despite the fact that the population had not increased to any vast extent.

In 1834 the long-awaited Poor Law Amendment Act came into effect. It laid down that no 'outdoor' relief was to be given to the able-bodied poor; in other words they had to go into the workhouse. This meant uncomfortable surroundings, and loss of personal freedom, plus the sense of shame which lingered on, in regard to these establishments, well into the twentieth century. The harshness was intended to serve as a deterrent. The workhouse conditions were similar to those of a prison, or at least a school; at first families were even separated from each other into the sexes, parents from children, husbands from wives, so that elderly couples might die without ever seeing each other again once they entered its portals. The inmates were told when to get up in the morning, and when to go to bed, and, of course, there was to be no smoking or drinking.

In addition, no proper provision was made for the sick, the aged or the very young, who were normally all herded in together. This was not intentional; it was just that it was far beyond the means of most parishes or even Unions to provide two or three sets of buildings. Nor was any allowance made for seasonal employment, resulting in sizeable variations in the number of able-bodied poor for which the parish or Union had to cater.

With the coming of the railways, however, and a gradual rise in travel and industrial production, new jobs were created, and more and more flexibility was applied to the interpretation of the Settlement Law.

It would be wrong to imagine that all our ancestors from Tudor until modern times were little more than serfs tied to the soil of their native parishes. At all times, there have been people who have had the money, the education or brainpower, the skills or talents, or maybe the sheer charm to enable them to make their way in the world.

Roman Catholics

What about those who played no part in the life of the parish, those who were not members of the Church of England or its associated Churches in Ireland, Scotland and Wales. How did they fare, and where can they be found on record? The most obvious and long-lasting of the other religious groups, at least if one leaves aside for a moment the Jews, is the Roman Catholics. Persecution against them started almost immediately after the Reformation in England, and continued for several centuries. It must be borne in mind that Catholicism was not some strange religion, invented by foreigners (which is how the majority of our ancestors probably viewed it) but the Old Religion to which everyone belonged before Henry VIII came upon the scene.

Catholics were persecuted for several reasons, chiefly were these: a fear and mistrust of foreign Catholic powers such as France and Spain; a loyalty towards all things English, including the Church of England; and the common assumption that anything which is different must automatically be wrong. Those who refused to attend their parish church were known as Recusants, a term which is usually synonymous with Roman Catholic. These Recusants furnished a considerable amount of income in the way of fines.

These were listed on 'Recusant Rolls'. Here is a presentation from Edgmond, Shropshire, for 1592:

> John Cherrington, Yeoman, fined £80 for that he hath not frequented the Parish Church of Edgmond, nor any other place of common prayers, there to remain in the time of prayer, at any time within the three months, but hath refrained himself from the same.

From the same county, this time from Newport for the years 1638–9, 1641–2 and 1644, we find:

> James Blunt, Gentleman. Half his lands in Hinstock seized by the King on account of his recusancy. Fined £60 and £13 for his goods.

The Protestation Returns

In 1641–2, with the country on the brink of the Civil Wars, Parliament undertook a form of protest against the imposition of what they saw as 'an arbitrary and tyrannical government'. Their representatives travelled through the country and collected signatures on documents which came to be called Protestation Returns. Not all these Returns have survived, those that still exist being housed in the Record Office of the House of Lords. Some printed copies have been produced and are to be found in CROs and libraries. Among the counties which have exceptionally good copies available, one should mention Cornwall, Devon, Dorset, Oxfordshire and Somerset. Among those originals known to be lost are those of Derbyshire, Leicestershire, Norfolk, and parts of Essex. Apart from isolated copies which have come to light in the parish registers of a few places in these counties, their contents have been lost for ever, unless more copies are discovered among parish records.

Not all the Returns for other counties still exist, and so it is worth while consulting the Society of Genealogists' Leaflet No 8, *The Protestation Returns of 1641–2. A Checklist of Printed and Other Sources*. The Returns represent a sort of census of all adult males for the years 1641–2 and, as such, represent a very important source of information for family historians. Although, basically, adult males were the only people invited

Protestation Return, Stonesfield, Oxon, listing all male members of the Parish in 1641. (*Courtesy of the Clerk of Record Office of the House of Lords*)

Stukeley in romn[...]
Dion   A list of all those wch haue taken the
                                     protestation

                                                                    144

Hen: Abbu Cunst

Robert Loten Churdwar[n]
Richard Holloway — wardens
John Dow
Will Lardner wolloth
John Morris Const
william Girill
George weston
Will the sonne of Robt Lardner
John Bushe
Thomas Dowre
william Horne
Will woolbridge
Will Hedges
John Hedges
Thomas Hedges
Edward Couper
Robt Janner
Robt Boxe
John Rowell
James Loten
John Loten
Thomas Loten
John House seni
Thomas Smith
Hugh Kirke
Nicholas Kirke
John Kirke
George Haish
Richard Kettes

Hen: Abbu Cunst
John Morris Constable
        his   marke
Roberte L   Langhton
        his   marke
Richard   D Holloway
  his and the
Churchwardens

Richard wise
william Lardner send of Doggats
Edward Lardner
Richard Lardner
James Lardner
Hugh Lardner
Robt Osbourne
John Osbourne
Richard Osbourne
Thomas Boulton
Daniell Boulton
Thomas White
John Dowse senr
John Burge
John Hedges
Will Lardner sen of Lincolns
Will Lardner jun of Lincolns
Richard Baldwin
Robt Tanner
Thomas Hollows
Ralph Greene
Robt stray
Thomas Greene
Richard Greene
william Swaine

Refusers none.

John Dowse

william D Lardner
        his   marke
Overseers

to sign, some women signed along with their husbands, and not all the male signatories were really adult as no birth certificates existed to be checked. In any case, the collectors were sure to have been glad of more, rather than fewer, signatures.

The signatures themselves are arranged under the unit of administration known as the Hundred, and then under the towns and villages which belonged to them. You may find an ancestor or another branch of the family residing several villages away, and so be put onto the trail in another set of registers. Often 'Sr' and 'Jr' are put after a name, suggesting that there are two generations to be found.

Everyone in the town or village had to be accounted for, and so, along with the sick and infirm who were unable to come and sign, we find our Recusants once again. Usually these last are stated as having refused to sign for religious reasons, although some Catholics are probably to be found among the invalids too.

The Protestation Returns, then, are useful not only because they allow one to establish where an ancestor was in 1641–2, but also because they give some idea of whether or not he was an adult at this time, and also of whether he was a declared Roman Catholic. If the latter is indeed the case, you need not waste time searching through parish registers for entries which may never be found there.

By the year 1657 anti-Catholic feeling had gone as far as to prompt the introduction of an Act which decreed that everyone must swear an oath against the Pope's authority. Those who refused to do so were presented at the Quarter Sessions. So, if you believe that your family may have remained Catholic after the Reformation, and hundreds of people did, especially in the north-west of England, you are likely to trace them as rebels and law-breakers, as, according to the legislation of the time, this is exactly what they were. It was not until the First Catholic Relief Act of 1778 that Catholic parishes truly came into being, although unofficial communities had formed themselves into informal parishes well before that date.

Present-day parishes are listed in the Catholic Directory, which has appeared annually since 1845, while the registers

146

have not been deposited but remain with the parish priest. However, the Catholic Record Society has published copies of registers and records from the sixteenth century onwards. There is a Catholic Central Library in Francis Street, London SW1, near Westminster Cathedral.

Non-conformists

'Non-conformist' is an overall term used to describe those Protestants of varying beliefs who refuse to accept the authority of the Church of England or its associated Church in Ireland, Scotland and Wales. Most Non-conformist bodies came into being in the seventeenth and eighteenth centuries, when they found that the teachings of the Established Church were not totally compatible with their own beliefs. Some were extreme or eccentric, and have not survived to this day, while others taught a humane and straightforward approach to Christian life.

The Act of Toleration of 1689, under William and Mary, decreed that dissenters were henceforth to be allowed to stay away from the parish church and use their own chapels and churches instead, without breaking the law, provided that they took the new oath of Allegiance and Supremacy, and accepted certain doctrines. Their places of worship were to be registered, and their services to be held without locked doors. The Quakers, however, would take no such oath, but were instead permitted to undertake a declaration of fidelity to the Government and a profession of belief in the Christian faith.

Presbyterians Presbyterianism originated with followers of Calvin who felt a need to return to a 'primitive' church, more, they believed, like the early Christian church would have been. In Scotland its actual tenets were expounded by John Knox in 1560, and it became the established church in Scotland in 1696. In 1875 a Pan-Presbyterian alliance was formed, and includes all churches in the United Kingdom, the United States, and world-wide.

The Presbyterian Church is a Protestant denomination, based on government by Church elders instead of by bishops and other clergy. All Church members have equal status, and live by a strict code of behaviour. Policy is determined by means of a system of presbyteries (or bodies of elders) synods (religious councils) and general assemblies.

Although, to English people, Presbyterianism is principally a Scottish denomination, English registers exist for most counties, mainly from the period covering the late-sixteenth to mid-eighteenth centuries, and are housed in the Public Record Office in Chancery Lane.

Unitarians are a Congregationalist sect which originated in the seventeenth century with the Presbyterians. The outstanding Unitarian belief is in the rejection of the Trinity in favour of the 'one-ness' of God. In 1928 the General Assembly of Unitarians and Free Christian Churches was formed. Old Unitarian registers are in the Public Record Office, the earliest examples being for Lancashire (1762) Staffordshire (1788) and Yorkshire (1817).

Of the various sects which come under the heading of Non-conformist, the *Baptists* are unique in that they maintained that only believers should be baptised, ie adults who had had time to make up their minds about the matter, and knew what they were doing. Baptism in infancy, therefore, was out of the question. Another feature of the Baptists was that they baptise by total immersion. One of the best-known Baptists is John Bunyan, who suffered for his beliefs by imprisonment in Bedford Gaol, where he managed to write *Pilgrim's Progress*.

The Baptists were split into two divisions: General Baptists, who believed that all believers would be saved; and Particular Baptists, who claimed that paradise was only open to God's chosen few. The General Baptists themselves split into two parts, the Old and New Connections, when the latter group was formed in 1770. When the Baptists' Union of 1813 brought them together once again, the Old Connection changed their name to Unitarians. In 1891 the New Connection and the Particulars merged.

We were never able to establish where, if anywhere, my father was christened; in fact, he himself had no idea. As he said, he would have been too young at the time to have had any recollection of the event! Questioning his older sisters was no use either; they also had no idea. Seventy years after the supposed event, no trace has yet been found and so we are forced to assume that it never did take place. We often wondered about this as all of his sisters had been christened in the same church, just outside Witney. The only conclusion that we could come to was that my paternal grandfather was a member of the Baptist Church (as was his father before him) and that his Church of England wedding, together with the subsequent christenings of his older children, had been a concession to his wife; or perhaps, as they all happened to be girls, it scarcely mattered to him. Maybe Grandad assumed that his only son would, in the fulness of time, be received into the Baptist Church in their adult baptism ceremony. If this was the case, he was sadly mistaken.

It never materialised because my father soon grew into a very independent small person, and no sooner had he left school than he promptly left home as well. Far from showing any interest in the various sects and denominations into which the family had divided itself – Baptists, Wesleyans, Anglicans and Salvationists – he studiously avoided all organised forms of religion whatsoever, the only exception being his own wedding.

This demonstrates just one of the numerous ways in which a baptismal entry can evade discovery; in this case it is no use blaming the vicar or the parish clerk as no amount of searching, however diligent, would have produced results.

The *Congregationalists* were against state invervention in any shape or form as regards religious matters, and were often known as Independents, although, strictly speaking, the term should be used for several sects together.

Congregationalists have produced a number of important educationalists and they took an active part in the founding of the University of London in the nineteenth century, and thus helped to break the dominance of Oxford and Cambridge, who only admitted members of the Established Church. In 1972, the Congregationalists joined forces with the Presbyterians to form the United Reformed Church.

A religious group which was founded in the seventeenth century, but rose to prominence in the eighteenth century was the Society of Friends, better known as the *Quakers*. They were the product of George Fox's endeavours to find a direct way of Christian worship, without what he considered unnecessary ritual. The early Quakers seem to have been quite revolutionary in their outlook, at least by the standards of the times, and they were therefore looked on as something of a threat to the quiet life of the community.

It is as record-keepers that the Quakers really come into their own, as far as the family historian is concerned. A clear and detailed picture of meeting-house life is given through the years. An index has been produced from pre-1837 Quaker registers, and contains some 500,000 names. It may be consulted at the Society of Friends' Central Repository (Friends House, Euston Road, London NW1).

The library there is open for research; an appointment is requested and there is a small hourly charge. The Society itself will do a certain amount of research, with a charge made for each hour's work. Some months delay is to be expected before any reply can be sent to enquirers.

The latest, and possibly the most widespread, of the Non-conformist denominations is *Methodism*. John Wesley's Society, which was formed in 1740 to reform certain aspects of the Church of England, became a separate denomination in its own right. It started at Oxford where John and his brother Charles were at university, and gradually became a worldwide movement. The Wesleys held their first meetings in college rooms and private houses, and some of the hymns which were the results of such services are among the best-loved today, thanks to the poetic and musical talents of the brothers.

Fairly early in its career Methodism split into several branches, which included the New Connexion (1797), the Primitive Connexion (1811), the Bible Christians (1815), the Primitive Methodists (1828) and the United Methodists' Free Church of 1857. These divisions reunited over the years, so that today the only separate branches are the Wesleyan Reform Union and the Independent Methodists. At the University of Manchester's John Ryland's Library can be found a large collection of Methodist material. In the same city is the Methodist Archives and Research Centre (c/o Property Division, Central Hall, Oldham Street, Manchester M1 1JQ). One useful publication (published by the Society of Genealogists) dealing with Methodism is entitled *My Ancestor was a Methodist; How can I Find More About Him?* A library which specialises in works on Non-conformity generally is Dr Williams' Library (14 Gordon Square, London WC1).

The *Salvation Army* was founded in 1865, by William Booth, with the dual aims of spreading the gospel and combatting the poverty and other social evils of the Victorian age, just as it endeavours to do today. Many people think of the Army as a musical as much as a religious organisation, a view brought about by its joyous, public hymn-singing, particularly at Christmas time when it plays and collects for charity. Salvationists are also justly famous for the wonderful work which they do among the under priviledged all over the world. It is this social work which engenders all the travelling which makes keeping track of Salvationist ancestors difficult if contact with that branch of the family is already lost.

Members of my own family left Oxfordshire to work with the Army in North America; one of them, the brother of Fred, who wrote the poem reproduced at the end of Chapter 3, was to become the father of Edith Garland, one of the 'stars' of Chapter 3. Edith treasures George's diary, in which he kept an account of his Salvationist activities at the close of the last century. One of the most interesting of these, at least to the outsider, found its way into the columns of the *Macomb Eagle*, an Illinois newspaper, in 1892. George, in an excess of enthusiasm, and in the none-too-desirable company of an individual known as Joe the Turk, managed to get himself locked away in the local jail, serving 'Fourteen Days for Jesus' as the paper's heading puts it, when describing this breaker of the Macomb peace. I still have an original copy of the *Eagle*, together with a photograph of 'Jailbird George', as he is known in the family to this day. As for George's wife, Edith's mother, I will let Edith herself explain:

> Mother came at 18, with the Salvation Army, to work as a "Slum Sister" in New York. This was in 1893. She travelled widely with a Colonel Blanch Cox, all over the States, soliciting funds for women's work. Mother was very good-looking, and had a nice soprano voice, so she provided the entertainment part of the lectures. Singing songs like "The Last Rose of Summer", and scattering rose petals as she sang. How corny can you get, but it was very popular, especially in the west, where miners threw silver dollars at her. She said they hurt. She met my father somewhere on these western jaunts, and they were married in Newark, N.J., on December 21, 1898.

I also possess a collection of picture postcards, and birthday and Christmas cards sent and received by Salvationist relatives all over the USA, Canada and Britain, many of them showing Salvationist flags, Temples and Citadels. Recently I was given a copy of a wedding invitation to the marriage of Edith Marie Ivings to Capt Herbert Mansfield Garland, at 8 pm, on 28 June 1928, in the Washington Temple Auditorium, the ceremony being conducted by another relative, Lt-Col William Barrett.

The Salvation Army has an International Heritage Centre at 117–121 Judd Street, London WC1H 9NN. Most records relating to the Army's local evangelistic and community work, however, are kept locally by corps and divisional headquarters, but the Centre holds many publications containing articles referring to local officers and soldiers; additional material is added constantly.

By far the majority of members of Non-conformist sects were normal, respectable people who lived side by side with their Anglican neighbours without attracting undue attention, beyond something of a reputation for eccentricity perhaps. Occasionally, however, trouble erupted when religious fanatics exceeded what was considered acceptable behaviour in such matters, usually where public morals were outraged, or when public money was involved. Such a case arose in October 1825 when the parishioners of St Thomas the Martyr, in a poor, working-class area to which newcomers to the city came to find accommodation which they could afford, decided that they had had enough of certain anti-social behaviour by members of their community:

Some of the superstitious followers of Mr. Mullock met with very rough treatment in this city on Thursday last.

Within the last week or ten days, three of the fanatics who associate with this man have actually separated themselves from their wives and families (with whom they had lived for years happily) under the idea that such a connection was contrary to the law of God.

Their families have applied to the Magistrate for assistance. The good women of St. Thomas's parish where one of these discarded wives lived, did not approve of this doctrine of separation, and, accordingly, on Thursday last when a party of the elect had assembled in the house of a man named Gardner, the mob broke the window and door, and destroyed a great part of the furniture. Mr. Mullock was not present at the meeting but his party was hooted through the streets and assailed with all sorts of mud and filth, their clothes torn and their features so much disfigured as to render it difficult to recognise them.

Mr. Hunt, chemist, at whose house the meetings were generally held, appears to have come in for an extra share of their favours; he was obliged to take shelter in the Town Hall yard until the mob had in some measure dispersed.

(Jackson's Oxford Journal, 8 October 1825)

Because of all the divisions, and the specialised beliefs of the particular branches of each denomination, those interested in any Non-conformist church would be well advised to contact the local Minister of the church in the first instance. He should be able to clarify any confusing points, and to tell you how best to find registers and records.

The policy for depositing registers varies from body to body, but, as a general rule, most were deposited either in the Public Record Office or the County one.

Quaker registers were deposited with the Registrar General after 1837, and are now in the Public Record Office. Other leading denominations which deposited their registers in the PRO are the majority of the Baptists, Congregationalists, Presbyterians and Unitarians. Also to be found there are those of some obscure sects, many of which have virtually died out. These include the Countess of Huntingdon's Connexion, the Inghamites, the Irvingites, the Moravians, the New Jerusalemites and the Swedenborgians.

Having given a brief outline of Non-conformity, it is now time to turn to what would probably nowadays be called the ethnic minorities who came to settle in this country, bringing with them their own religious practices. Two of these in particular, made a considerable contribution to our society and economy; these were the Jews and the Huguenots.

Jews probably first settled here in any numbers under the early Norman kings, and it is known that they were granted a charter by Henry I. In the Middle Ages the most important Jewries were those of Bristol, Canterbury, Gloucester, Lincoln, London, Northampton, Norwich and York, although, as the street names Jewry and Old Jewry indicate, there were Jews living in most towns of any size. Because, in theory, Christians were not permitted by their religion to act as money-lenders, Jews found a thriving business theirs for the

153

asking. Soon a large number of influential Englishmen, together with many of their countrymen, were in debt to Jewish lenders and some of them began to resent the obligation which they were under. If the Jews were expelled, said a little voice in the nation's ear, they would take the debts with them. This upsurge of anti-Semitic feeling, which was exacerbated by a certain amount of jealousy, was encouraged by the Church as a just punishment for the race which had killed Christ. It was all very righteous in tone, and also very convenient. Public feeling eventually led to the expulsion of the Jews in 1290, but not before they had suffered a considerable amount of persecution.

Nearly 400 years later, Oliver Cromwell encouraged Jewish merchants and businessmen to settle in England and bring their wealth with them. Since the seventeenth century a steady stream of Jewish immigrants has come to this country, often after persecution abroad. This brought about the re-establishment of sizeable Jewish communities once again, all over Britain. Although, as a rule, they did not, in the past, intermarry or enter into any aspects of parish life, they made a vast contribution to the commercial and political life of the country, and even produced a Prime Minister.

Jewish wills and administrations are to be found detailed in the *Anglo-Jewish Notabilities* produced by the Jewish Historical Society of England. Another source of help is the Anglo-Jewish Association (Woburn House, Upper Woburn Place, London WC1). The Jewish Museum is also at the above address and is worth a visit by anyone, Jewish or not, who is interested in Judaism.

Large-scale immigration to this country during the last century, and an attempt to fit in with the native population, persuaded many people with Jewish surnames which the British find difficult, or who simply wished to conceal their origins, to alter them to something a little more English-sounding. Many 'bergs' and 'steins' were dropped in the process, and so, if it seems that the surname in which you are interested may not reveal the whole truth about its beginnings, try consulting the Returns of Aliens and naturalisation papers, as well as Certificates of Entry. The latter two are to be found at the Public Record Office at Kew with the Home Office papers, while Returns of Aliens were registers kept by Justices of the Peace. An alien had to register with the Justices, according to the legislation passed in 1792, and give his or her name, address, rank and occupation. Furthermore, private citizens who had aliens in their houses were supposed to give notice of the fact to the parish authorities, who, in turn, made returns which they sent to the Clerk of the Peace. Once again, try the appropriate CRO. Needless to say, plenty of people simply changed their names informally, or were known by nicknames, without bothering to do anything legally, and of these there will be little or no record. Another Society of Genealogists publication, *My Ancestor Was Jewish: Can I Find More About Him?*, may well prove of use.

Old Jewish registers were not deposited with the Public Record Office. Those from 1687 to 1837 are kept at the Bevis Marks Synagogue, in London EC3. It is also a good idea to approach the Rabbi or Secretary for Marriages of your local synagogue if you are not of the Jewish faith and need some help or explanation.

The *Huguenots* were French Protestants, persecuted in their native country, who fled abroad. The majority settled in the Netherlands, but an estimated 40,000 found their way here, to live chiefly in London, Kent, Sussex, Norfolk and Bristol, after the Revocation of the Edict of Nantes in 1685, which meant that they could no longer enjoy freedom of worship in France. Huguenots had been arriving in this country, however, throughout the sixteenth and seventeenth centuries, whenever they were threatened in France; in theory at least, about three-quarters of all English people could have some Huguenot blood, so well did they integrate into the host community.

Not only did they settle well with their English neighbours, they also brought with them wealth, business acumen and great artistic talent. Many were leading craftsmen, and English woodwork, silver, scientific instruments and the textile industry, to name but a few of their activities, owe an enormous debt to Huguenot workmanship. An article in the September 1985 edition of *Reader's Digest*, 'Our Huguenot Connexion', by John Harman, states that our Princes William and Harry have no fewer than fifteen proven lines of Huguenot descent. Other famous people with Huguenot blood include Lord Olivier, Sir Winston Churchill (on his mother's side),

Roget of *Thesaurus* fame, and the Courtauld family. Any French-sounding surname may be of Huguenot origin, as well as many more which have been either anglicised or directly translated. Of course not all French names are necessarily Huguenot in origin; many came from individual French settlers here, or via the Channel Islands, while yet others may be common to both England and France and differ only in pronunciation.

The Huguenot Society (which may be contacted through Barclay's Bank Plc, Pall Mall, London SW1) has produced lists of applicants for naturalisation, 1509–1800. They have made copies, too, of the older Huguenot original registers which are now in the Public Record Office.

The subject of this chapter, parish life, is not a particularly easy one for the family historian to make his or her way through, bogged down as it is by Bills, Acts and dates. It is this very legislation, though, which provides a means for us to find out more details about our ancestors, whether or not they were active participants in the life of their parish. If, on the other hand, they preferred to make alternative arrangements for the practising of their religious beliefs, and the squaring of their consciences at the expense of their place in the community, we shall also be able, in many cases, to find them doing just that and accepting the consequences.

9
Death and Burial

Causes of death

Our ancestors were killed by most of the current slayers of humankind (although, in those days, they sometimes masqueraded under different, and more exotic, names) and also by plenty more which we have now succeeded in combatting. The most infamous, of course, were the Black Death, which swept through fourteenth-century Europe, and the Great Plague of 1665, but countless minor attacks of plague broke out throughout the country, and are duly recorded in parish registers.

Apart from the more obvious diseases and afflictions – smallpox, diphtheria, consumption and cholera, for example – our forebears were also vicitims of what we now term mere childhood ailments. Wasting diseases and 'fading' sicknesses (cancers) also took their toll, as did syphilis, 'the stone', and suppression of urine, plus assorted bloatings, swellings and burstings. Other tragedies gleaned from burial records include being trampled by farmyard animals, starvation, and adverse weather conditions, which included being struck by lightning. Related to lightning were lunacy, and the more picturesque 'visitations' and 'acts of God'. These last were probably a polite way of indicating that the medical men of the time had either no idea of what the deceased had contracted, or else had actually hastened his demise themselves by the treatment which he had received at their hands. Death, then, was often sudden and sometimes inexplicable, as this parish-register entry from Blymhill, Staffordshire (dated 28 July 1817) shows:

Hannah Humpage, Brineton, aged 54 buried. Note. This woman, without a minute's illness, while she was making hay, fell down and, without uttering a word, expired immediately. Whoever thou art who readest this, prepare to meet thy God.

157

Many afflictions might have been prevented by rudimentary hygiene and sanitary arrangements, but these were a subject far from the hearts and minds of the average Englishman until well into the nineteenth century. Poor diet and unsuitable eating habits also played their parts in making the human body a fine breeding-ground for viruses and disease. It has been estimated that in Jane Austen's day (1775–1817) the average female life expectancy was somewhere in the region of thirty-five years. Small wonder, then, that her heroines and their mothers were so concerned with contracting suitable marriages before time ran out on them. Viewed in this light, the above-mentioned Hannah Humpage was already living on borrowed time.

By the middle of the nineteenth century industrialisation had drawn thousands of families away from the country villages where they had lived and worked for generations, into the inner-city areas, which were fast turning into slums. Although the death rate had dropped from approximately 1 in 40 to 1 in 60 (mainly as a result of the conquest of smallpox and the reduction in deaths from outright starvation), what we now consider an unacceptably high rate of infant mortality was regarded as inevitable until the present century. Open up any burial register at random, and you will find a distressing number of babies' funerals recorded, pathetic little creatures, many of them only months, weeks or even hours old. Some were unbaptised and therefore disposed of in unconsecrated ground, much to the anguish of the already sorrowing parents.

As a percentage of the total deaths for 1897, according to the report of the Registrar General, the figure for those dying aged less than one year varied from 25 per cent, in an agricultural county such as Herefordshire, to nearly double that figure, 46 per cent, in the Black Country. As recently as 1911, the year of the National Insurance Act, the mortality rate for the children of manual workers was estimated at 15 per cent, as opposed to 7.6 per cent for those of middle- and upper-class parentage.

Disposal of the remains:

Strange and – to us at least – horrible things were likely to happen to our ancestors when they died. The higher their rank, the more liable their corpses were to be mutilated.

We are familiar with the idea of embalming a dead body, but members of the royal family or the aristocracy who died away from home were often dismembered and boiled down, after which their bones were taken to be cleaned off ready for transporting to the family estate. So strong was the territorial instinct, and the desire to lie in one's own earth, that many corpses received this treatment, one of them being that of Henry V, who was unlucky enough to die in France and whose remains were brought back to England for a state funeral in Westminster Abbey.

Medieval people were very conscious of the fact that death was just around the corner, and they were constantly being exposed to evidence of this fact. The obsession with mortality and the decay of the flesh reached its peak towards the end of the fifteenth century with an outbreak of paintings, frescoes and murals depicting the 'Dance of Death', the 'Living and the Dead', the 'Day of Judgement', and numerous other reminders that the occupants of the tomb were once just as the onlooker is now, and that he or she will soon become as they are.

Particularly macabre are the effigies which show the deceased as a decomposing corpse, complete with worms, and frequently sporting an only too realistic scar like the lacing of a football, reaching across the abdomen. This scar was left after certain internal organs had been removed prior to embalming. Not surprisingly, the process of embalming was in itself a rather hazardous occupation, and more than one practitioner is known to have died of infection from a less than fresh subject.

Many people will have heard the story of how Robert the Bruce's heart was taken out and put into a casket, in readiness for transportation to the Holy Land. Others who similarly lost their hearts include Aymer de Valance, who has a little heart-shrine in Winchester Cathedral, and the great Montrose, whose heart, nestling in a little silver casket, made its way to India before it was discovered, brought home again, and subsequently lost once more.

Lesser mortals, too, had parts of their anatomy removed before burial. These usually consisted of the heart and viscera, which were then deposited in urns and niches in chancel walls. They earned their own places in the burial register. Thus from

Woodstock, Oxfordshire, we find this entry (dated 30 September 1670): 'The bowells of Lord Lovlass were buried in Woodstock Church.' In 1702, the same parish gives us: 'The Bowels of Henry Meux of Pagham in the Isle of Wight interred.' This Mr Meux was a former curate, and, one assumes, the rest of the reverend gentleman returned home to the Isle of Wight.

It is unlikely that you will ever have the unnerving experience of coming across your ancestor portrayed as a mouldering corpse, or find a memorial inscription on an urn containing his bowels, but it just could happen. A great number of our forebears, on the other hand, went to their graves clad only in a shroud knotted at head and foot, and with no lasting memorial, save for the descendants who bear their name.

One parishioner who would have taken up much more than her fair share of the churchyard was Mrs Dodd, who died in January 1765, in St Ebbe's parish, Oxford. This report is from *Jackson's Oxford Journal*.

Last Monday died in Pennyfarthing Street Mrs. Dodd, widow of Charles Dodd, Taylor, who was probably the most bulky woman of her stature in England, being rather short in her person, and yet said to weigh over 4 cwt. She had been extremely fat for many years before her marriage but has, notwithstanding, had several children, and was so much inclined to think herself pregnant during her last illness as to desire that her body might be opened after her Decease.

However, we believe Mrs. Dodd was mistaken in her conjectures. She had been decrepit in her legs and so unwieldy as to be unable to walk about. Her Bulk was almost incredible since her arm measured no less than 27 inches round, and her body proportionally larger.

Her coffin was 3' 6" wide and 19" deep.

An unusual form of demise sometimes found the deceased a mention in the newspapers. Here is an extract from the report of an inquest on one Mrs Seabright, who dropped dead very suddenly in 1829. The witness is Mary Sylvester, a longstanding friend of Mrs. Seabright:

I was at Mrs. Seabright's house at 11 o'clock yesterday morning;

she was in good health. I was accustomed to sleep at Mrs. Seabright's when I was out of a place and used to leave my clothes there.

When I called on Tuesday morning, I asked Mrs. Seabright for the things I had left, and she gave me a petticoat, a nightcap, and a pocket handkerchief.

I said "Mrs. Seabright, you have not given me one of my caps." She said she had not got it there.

I replied "I saw it on the table when I was here last." Mrs. Seabright then said "I wish God may strike me dead and I may never move out of the house any more if I have it!"

I then left her in the house and went into the house next-door-but-one, and in less than ten minutes after I had left, Mrs. Randall, who lives in the adjoining house, called me into Mrs. Seabright's. I accordingly went, and caught Mrs. Seabright as she was falling. She said, "Oh Mary!" several times and asked me to help her upstairs. I tried, but was not able, as she was so heavy. She died the same evening.

Graves

A respectable burial was felt to be highly desirable by all classes of society. Even if one had led a somewhat rough life, a good departure was deemed necessary. A pauper funeral, paid for by the parish, was a disgrace to be avoided wherever possible, not only because its cost was entered into the parish records for all to see, but also because the treatment of the deceased left much to be desired. The parish coffin might be used, or else a cheap version which threatened to disintegrate before it was even lowered into the grave.

Inner-city parishes, where burial space was at a premium, sometimes adopted the policy of making a common grave for paupers. In cases of serious shortage of space, the grave might be left open as long as there was still room for just one more body to fit in it. The resultant stench from the first-comers must have been too dreadful to think about.

The funeral of an artisan in the mid-nineteenth century was liable to cost his family something in the region of £5, while a middle-class burial, complete with all the show and ritual, would have left little change from £100.

Pamela Keegan observed a set of burial patterns in the churchyard of the small north Oxfordshire village of Cropredy, and wrote an account of them in her article entitled

161

'Cropredy' in the *Oxfordshire Family Historian*, volume 1, number 4, spring 1978:

> ... a pattern emerged of trade groups. To the west of the tower are many Butchers, and Farmers. On a triangular patch to the south, a family of Plumbers and Glaziers predominate. A line of Harness-makers are near the south porch, and further south-east a large area of Millers, backed to the east by Yeomen. On the north side are the Cordwainers and Wheelwrights. The former families are opposite their family house in Red Lion Street and the latter are relatives and descendants of the innkeeper of the Red Lion Inn.

Even the more prosperous middle and upper classes, however, were not guaranteed a permanent and undisturbed resting-place, either inside or outside the church. Grave-robbers, and the constant dread of ending up on an anatomist's table in the medical schools, were a worry. One would expect to be left in peace away from all interferences in the church itself, but here is Pepys on the death of his brother, Tom, in 1664:

> So to the church, and with the grave-maker chose a place for my brother to lie in, just under my mother's pew. But to see how a man's tombes are at the mercy of such a fellow, that for sixpence he would (as his owne words were) "I will justle them together but I will make room for him", speaking of the fulness of the middle isle, where he was to lie.

Here is the *Jackson's Oxford Journal* once again, this time on the subject of grave-robbing:

> This week a set of Abandoned Miscreants were discovered in an attempt to rob a grave in Magdalen Parish Churchyard in this City, in which the bodies of a woman and Infant had been interred two nights before. They were alarmed just as they were going to break the ground, upon which they took to their Heels and the bodies were next day taken up and re-interred in the Church to prevent any future attempt.

Cremation

In the United Kingdom cremation is a very recent development, although it has been practised for centuries in

DEATH AND BURIAL

other cultures. The first British Cremation Society was not
formed until 1874, and, after a series of campaigns during the
1870s and 80s, the practice was finally made legal in 1884.
Even then there was a great deal of opposition, both from the
Church and the general public. More than one early cremation
needed a police escort before it could take place.

In 1963 papal authority was finally obtained for Roman
Catholics to be cremated, but, even today, many Catholics,
together with orthodox Jews and Muslims, believe cremation
to be wrong. Its critics argue that problems will arise on the
Day of Resurrection, when we will all be assembled round the
throne of God, and our bodies will be needed once more. To
this theory a pro-cremationist retorted that, if this were indeed
the case, what would happen about the martyrs who had been
burned at the stake?

Whatever one's personal feelings, thousands of people have
been cremated over the course of the last century. A
publication obtainable from the Society of Genealogists which
might prove useful is *Greater London Cemeteries and
Crematoria and their Registers*, and, of course, provincial
crematoria keep their own records.

In many churchyards there is a section set aside for the
burial of ashes, each with its own little headstone, and looking
for all the world like an infant's grave.

Memorial inscriptions

In connection with memorials one should mention that, all
over the country, public-spirited local and family-history
society members are working hard to preserve and record
inscriptions. Their findings are usually made available to all in
County Record Offices and central libraries.

Memorials to members of the upper classes and better-off
professional and tradespeople may take the form of a stone
tomb or a plaque, slab or brass, or even a stained-glass
window inside the church. The overwhelming majority of
memorials, however, were simply plain wooden crosses which
rotted along with the bodies under them. Some seventeenth
century gravestones have survived, but the greater part date
from later centuries, and many have been badly damaged by
time and the weather.

When looking for memorial inscriptions, do not confine your attentions to the parish churchyard. Bear in mind also the hundreds of chapels-of-ease and Non-conformist burial grounds, whether you are looking for the inscriptions themselves, or for copies of them in the comfort of a warm office or library. Many collections are arranged under the individual church or chapel, while others appear under county or town.

Some inscriptions are very basic, while others are a mine of information, perhaps giving details of one or two generations. Some are unintentionally amusing, such as this one from an Edinburgh Kirkyard: 'Erected to the Memory of John McFarlane Drownd in the Water of Leith by a few affectionate friends'. A second Scottish example comes from Inverskip Street, Greenock, and says with Scottish thoroughness:

John Dunlop tide surveyor [died] 1.1.1805 [aged] 75, son of Alexander, professor [of] greek [at] Glasgow university. Son of principal Dunlop and nephew of principal Carstairs, sister Sarah Dunlop [died] 4.4.1805 [aged] 87, brother Hutcheson Dunlop, major 53rd Regiment Foot [died] – 5.1790 [aged] 45. Wife Jean Fisher [died] – 3.1817 [aged] 79, daughter of Rev. Fisher, minister, Maybole, son Alexander merchant here now of Keppoch, wife Janet Graham [died] 7.6.1795 [aged] 26, son Henery Liston Dunlop [died] 10.5.1808 [aged] 17, daughter Robina Liston Dunlop [died] – 8.1816 [aged] 3, son John, writer here whose children: son 1819 [died in] infancy, Margaret Jean [died] 6.9.1833 [aged] 16, daughter Mary Janet [died] 23.2.1834.

Deaths in the parish register

The last-mentioned inscription gives an almost instant family tree, but, sooner or later, everyone will have to turn to the research of parish registers. These often only give bare essentials, at least until the nineteenth century, when details were given on death certificates and record-keepers became more forthcoming.

Until that time one is lucky if one can manage to distinguish between generations, and even families, with the same names. The average burial entry is likely to state baldly that, on 17 December 1755 Henry Brown was buried. Now which of our Henrys, father, son, cousin or grandson, do we take this to refer to? If the age of the deceased is of any interest to the writer he may jot down the odd word of description, such as 'yonge man', 'mayden' or 'aged', or even the parents of a dead infant. He may go as far as labelling the deceased as 'senior' or 'junior', 'widow' or 'widower', mentioning the relevant spouse, and give the occupation and part of the parish in which they lived. This bonus, is, unfortunately, not to be taken for granted, and the plain 'buried Henry Brown' is quite normal.

Occasionally one will end up with a surfeit of Henrys, one or two more being buried than appear to have been baptised or married in the parish. In this case you will probably be dealing with relatives moving into the village from elsewhere, possibly to find work or live with their children in their old age.

Normally, though, one must be prepared to do some calculations, and attempt a little inspired guesswork. Worth trying are checking the baptism of the last recorded child, whether the ancestor in question was old enough to have signed the Protestation Returns of 1641–2 (that is, about eighteen at that date) and, with later marriages, whether or not the bride or groom's father is noted as deceased.

On a more general level, burial registers can tell you quite a lot about the social history of the parish; how many children were lost; how many wives died in childbirth; whether it was acceptable to marry again within a certain period of time; how many incomers – soldiers, perhaps, or travellers – died there while passing through, and, as already mentioned, a list of all the fascinating things that human flesh is prone to and the ailments to which our ancestors succumbed.

While researching burial registers, one may come across the words 'affidavit received' (or, more commonly, an abbreviation, such as 'aff't rc'd'), which are to be found after burial entries from the 1660s until the beginning of the nineteenth century.

The affidavit was a statement sworn in front of a magistrate to the effect that a corpse had been buried in wool, and thus complied with an Act passed in 1667, and more strictly enforced from 1678 onwards, in order to help the ailing English woollen industry. The penalty for burial in a material which was not pure wool was £5. This Burial in Woollen Act did 'enjoyne that they are not to be buried in any shirt, shift, sheet or shroud made or mingled with flax, hemp, silk, hair,

John Osborn of the Parish of *St Sepulchers* in the *City* of *London* maketh Oath, That *Mrs Sarah Gold* of the Parish of *St Dunstan West* in the *City of London* lately Deceased, was not put in, wrapt, or wound up, or buried in any Shirt, Shift, Sheet, or Shroud, made or mingled with Flax, Hemp, Silk, Hair, Gold, or Silver, or other than what is made of Sheeps Wool only; nor in any Coffin lined or faced with any Cloth, Stuff, or any other thing whatsoever made or mingled with Flax, Hemp, Silk, Hair, Gold or Silver, or any other Material, contrary to the late Act of Parliament for Burying in Woollen, but Sheeps Wool only. Dated the 20th Day of October in the Twelveth Year of the Reign of our Sovereign Lord, GEORGE II. by the Grace of God, of Great-Britain, France and Ireland, King, Defender of the Faith, &c. and in the Year of our Lord God, 1738

John Osborn

Sealed and Subscribed by us who were present, and Witnesses to the Swearing of the abovesaid Affidavit.

Henry Box

William Box

I *John Poulton Esqr* one of His Majesties Justices of the Peace for the said County of Midd do hereby Certifie, That the Day and Year abovesaid, the said *John Osborn* came before me and made such Affidavit, as is abovementioned, according to the said late Act of Parliament, Intituled, *An Act for Burying in Woollen*, Witness my Hand the Day and Year above-written.

Poulson

LONDON, Printed for, and Sold by JOSEPH MARSHALL, at the Bible in Newgate-street, where are sold, Bibles and Common prayers of all Sorts: Likewise Ink-powder, by wholesale or retale, and Japan-Ink at 6 d. a Bottle, and Funeral-Tickets, where Country Chapmen may be supplied; and with blank Receipts for the Land-Tax and Window-Lights.

gold, or silver or any other than what is made of sheep's wool'. Nearly everyone found it worth while to bury their dead in wool, and sign the affidavit to that effect, but now and again one comes across an entry such as the one from Beaconsfield in 1726 which states: 'buried in linen, penalty paid'. This particular entry is interesting as the family concerned was that

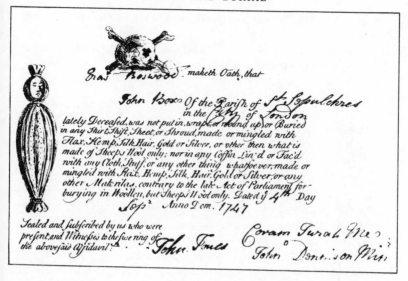

Affidavits for Burials in Woollen. Particularly graphic specimens from the collection of 894 owned by the parish of South Newington; the vast majority are simple and written by hand (*By kind permission of the Vicar, Rev Dr Edward Condry*)

of a local magistrate, in front of whom others swore their affidavits.

The Act was not repealed until 1814, by which year, however, it had already fallen into disuse.

Burials not taking place in the parish churchyard

Not everyone was able, or indeed willing, to be interred in the parish churchyard of their own town or village. Many Nonconformists preferred burial in one of the municipal cemeteries which had opened up round the country from the seventeenth century onwards. Such cemeteries kept their own burial registers, and among the leading ones should be noted those of London's Bunhill Fields (1713–1854), Walworth (South London) (1829–37) and Victoria Park (1853–76), Sheffield's Eccleshall (1836–8), one in Leeds (1835–7) and Liverpool's Everton (1825–37); the registers of which are in the Chancery Lane Building of the Public Record Office. Nor must we forget all the numerous smaller non-parochial burial-grounds, details of whose registers are likely to be found in the local County Record Office or central library.

Death also occurred in hospital and on board ship, whether Royal Navy or Merchant Navy. If you suspect that your ancestor could have perished in such circumstances, the Public Record Office can offer registers belonging to the Chelsea (1692–1856), Greenwich (1705–1857), Foundling and British Lying-In Hospitals. As for deaths on the ocean wave, St Catherine's House holds the registers for deaths on HM ships from 1837 until the present day, and on merchant ships from 1837 until 1874. For deaths on merchant ships occuring after this year, application should be made to the Registrar General for Shipping and Seamen, Llandaff, Cardiff.

Funeral Cards

Our forefathers were punctilious about the sending of funeral cards, not just the cards of condolence sent to the bereaved family such as we still send, but also cards sent by the family to friends and relations.

Funeral cards were usually about the size of a large gift-tag, were folded, and showed flowers if the deceased was a child or a woman, or a land- or seascape if male. Inside was a somewhat sentimental verse similar to those found in present-day 'In memoriam' columns, and sometimes a photograph of the deceased was included, together, of course, with the date and place of burial.

These cards have become something of collectors' items over the last few years, and the Museum of London has a fine collection, a display of which forms part of their exhibit illustrating the 'Victorian way of death'.

Death certificates

Like birth and marriage certificates, death certificates began with civil registration in 1837 in England and Wales (1855 for Scotland and 1864 in Ireland).

English and Welsh certificates are identical in that they give the name, address and age of the deceased, the cause of death and the name of the person providing the information, together with the latter's relationship, if any, to the deceased. Irish certificates, both from the Republic and Northern Ireland, are similar to Anglo-Welsh ones.

Copies of certificates are available locally from the office of the Superintendent Registrar of the district where the death took place, or centrally from the General Registrar's Office. In either case, the cost of a copy at the time of writing is £5.50 if making application in person. Until a few years ago it was necessary for the researcher to consult death indexes, not at St Catherine's House, but at Alexander house, also in Kingsway, (although the actual certificates could not be ordered there) but this, fortunately, is no longer the case. Today the death indexes are also at St Catherine's House along with all the others. Like most types of certificate, death certificates can be ordered by post, both locally and from St Catherine's House, but the fee charged will be double that of a personal application. If you possibly can, therefore, it is well worth while making the effort of presenting yourself at the appropriate office, or persuading a friend to go for you.

Scottish death certificates are of two types, those relevant to deaths in the initial year of registration (1855), and those for subsequent years. Those for 1855 are very detailed, so much so that they proved much too difficult to administer, and later certificates show less detail.

Scottish certificates of 1855 show the deceased's place of birth, the details of any marriages, the place of burial, and the names of all offspring alive or dead; all this is in addition to the usual information such as cause of death. These are wonderful acquisitions if your quarry was considerate enough to die in 1855, and if all the information is correct. This, unfortunately, is by no means always the case. It is easy to see how wrong information came to be given to the registrar, particularly in the case of an elderly person dying with no near relatives in the district, or if someone died a long way from where he or she was best known.

Current Scottish certificates are similar to those of the other British countries with the addition of details of the names of both parents of the deceased, and their mothers' maiden name. Death indexes are housed in the New Register House, Edinburgh. There is a charge for consulting them, but this fee allows one to look at the certificates themselves, and it is not therefore necessary to purchase a copy in order to see what information a certificate contains.

Irish death certificates are obtainable from the General Register Office (Oxford House, 49–55, Chichester Street, Belfast BT1 4HL), or, for the Republic of Ireland, from the Oifig an Ard-Chlaraitheora (in other words the Registrar General's Office, Joyce House, 8–11, Lombard Street East, Dublin 2).

Wills

In accordance with the Probate Act of 1857, all wills proved since that year in England and Wales, are kept at Somerset House in the Strand. It is a very simple matter to read them there, as one may walk straight in from the street, look up the name to be researched in the yearly indexes, and, if successful, fill in a request form for the will to be brought for your inspection.

There is a small charge, and an even smaller waiting period, dependent, of course, on demand. Should you prefer, you can ask for a copy of the will to be sent to your home address, on payment of a small fee.

Frequently it is not even necessary to see the will (although the conscientious researcher will, of course, require a copy for the family archives). The indexes themselves provide a useful source of information as they give the date and place of death. The latter, in particular, can sometimes prove surprising, and thus save a good deal of time, money and patience being spent on a fruitless search in the seemingly obvious area. In the past, as indeed today, the elderly often moved away from their home parishes to be with their children or grandchildren, or perhaps to go into a home or hospital to end their days.

Will indexes also give the names of executors, and an outline of the will's contents, so offering an inexpensive way of confirming a date of death, with the added bonus of obtaining addresses of certain family members at a given date.

Somerset House would seem to offer one of the best bargains in London. Compared with the death indexes at St Catherine's House, one has only to deal with yearly instead of quarterly volumes, the will is available on demand instead of one having to wait a matter of weeks for a certificate to arrive, and the cost involved is much smaller. Best of all, one can be certain that one is dealing with the right ancestor. Not everyone, naturally, made a will, but even if they did not, providing that they had money, land or property to be disposed of, the details of arrangements made for its administration after their death will appear in the indexes.

Before the Married Women's Property Act of 1882, it was not common for women to make wills unless they were spinsters or widows. Anything belonging to a married woman was considered to be her husband's property and, as such, was likely to appear in his will. As a consequence, wills made by females are comparatively rare, and those which exist were normally made by women in the above-mentioned categories, or else by women who were of higher social status than their husbands, perhaps by heiresses in their own right, for example.

Wills proved before 1858 are a different matter altogether from those to be found at Somerset House. Early wills are a fascinating but complex subject and one which would need a separate book to do it justice. Indeed, several have been written exclusively on the subject of wills, among which the two classics are J. S. W. Gibson's *Wills and Where to Find Them* and A. J. Camp's *Wills and their Whereabouts*. Both books should be readily available in any collection of family-history materials, and should be used to the full.

Until 1858 wills were normally proved in an ecclesiastical court, hence the pious (and, let us hope, sincere) preambles which are usually fairly lengthy and serve to introduce the body of the will itself. A typical example of such an introduction is this one from 1701:

> In the name of god Amen. I Richard ffountent of Skinnon in the County of Lincoln yeoman being sick of body but of good and perfect mind praised bee god for the same doe make and ordaine this my Last Will and testament in the manner and forme following viz first I bequeath my soule into the hands of Almighty god my Creator hopeing through the righteousness and mediation of his Son Jesus Christ my Redeemer to receive remission of sins and eternal life and I commit my body to the ground to bee decently buried by the descretion of my Executor and those wordly goods which it hath pleased god to give mee, I give and bequeath as followeth . . . .

This is a fairly restrained example; others were much more morbid, demonstrating an obsession with the decay and corruption of the mortal flesh quite worthy of our medieval ancestors. 'Houses of clay' are frequently mentioned, as are 'Earthly tabernacles of flesh'. Sometimes a testator went as far as to sign the will not only with his or her autograph or mark, but also with a finger- or thumb-print, usually in wax, but occasionally in blood. The marks made were normally a plain cross or initial, but now and again one finds something a little more imaginative such as a tailor signing with a tiny pair of scissors.

The main body of the will may consist of anything from the barest statement such as 'I leave all my wordly goods to my loving wife', without even a mention of her name, to a bewildering account of an assortment of legacies and debts to be repaid. Some people would appear to have died owing money to half the parish, together with a good few from surrounding ones, with a 'iid' (2d) here, and 'Viijd' (8d) there.

One soon becomes accustomed to the wide range of clothing which features in wills; the specific bequeathing of hose was not unknown, together with just about every other type of apparel. Margaret Fountent, of Navenby, Lincolnshire, of the same family as the aforementioned Richard, one presumes, in a will dated 1666, left to 'my daughter Margaret Blow my best gowne and my petticoat with the green lace off it and my hatt next my best hatt'. Mrs Fountent's will is interesting in that it is made by a widow, and the inheritors are also, in the main, female.

Furniture, household items and bedding (including the beds themselves, frequently 'the bed upon which I now lie') were very common bequests and feature prominently in both wills and inventories. Hempen sheets and brass 'potts' also play a large part, along with domestic animals, often sheep, and farm equipment. Even the smallest items were listed and valued for an inventory. One made upon the death of one Robert Hobson of Askham Bryan near York, in 1757, goes as far as listing the contents of the fold, namely 'Bean Stacks Helm Welltrough and Standlocks and Manure', all of which came to the princely sum of £9 10s twice the value of the Back Kitchen, which, with its 'One Table, Two Kettles, two brass panns, four stone of Lead, two churns and other Householdments' was worth a mere £4 15s.

The contents of the household, and their value and disposal, constitutes a fascinating source of social and economic history, whether or not one's own ancestors are mentioned, but it is the composition of the family itself which will prove the main attraction for the family historian. The ideal will, if such a thing can be said to exist, should tell us not only the occupation of the testator, the name of his or her spouse, children and other members of the immediate family, but also give details of sons- and daughters-in-law, brothers- and sisters-in-law, cousins, grandchildren and even great-grandchildren, and other interrelated families, plus something about the way of life and standard of living of them all.

Some wills, surprisingly, make no mention of a son (usually the eldest) whom one is sure was alive when the will was made. If he does not seem to have been provided for, this does not necessarily imply a quarrel or that any mistake has been made as regards dates. A likely reason is that he may have already received something in advance from the father's estate, possibly to start his own business or on marriage. Or the family may have made other arrangements for his future and thought it unnecessary to state the obvious in the will.

Incidentally, the date of the will is not necessarily near to that of death. Far-sighted people, together with the odd hypochondriac, would make their wills well in advance, perhaps at the birth of a grandson, or at the first serious twinges of middle-age. It has been said that Lowland Scots and Englishmen were well advised to make their wills before venturing into the Highlands in the days before the breakdown of the clan system, and this would have applied to other, less dangerous pursuits, such as signing on in the Army, or making a long sea journey.

Even those seemingly at death's door sometimes made spectacular recoveries, and there were always those who produced more children or grandchildren, or even remarried after making their wills, and never got round to altering them. Thus the actual date of the will is important for establishing the whereabouts of and relationships between the members of a family who appear in it, but, as a proof of date of death, the date of probate is a more accurate pointer.

As has already been stated, will-hunting is a complicated affair. The main points to bear in mind are that one needs to know both where the testator died, and where his or her property lay. If these were in different places, then probate was the responsibility of the higher ecclesiastical court of the two (or more) locations.

The lowest court in order of seniority was that of an archdeacon. If the property was situated in more than one archdeaconry, but within the same diocese, then the diocesan court came into action. If the property lay in two or more dioceses, but within the same ecclesiastical Province (ie of Canterbury or of York), then either the Prerogative Court of Canterbury (the PCC) or that of York (the PCY) would be responsible. When the property was situated in both Provinces, the PCC was the higher court, and therefore dealt with the will.

Until the Probate Act of 1857, then, the PCC was the highest probate authority in England, dealing with wills made by those who died abroad or at sea, as well as those in the circumstances mentioned above. Its records go back to 1383. Sometimes the PCC was used by those who had no need to do so, usually because they had social pretensions, or wished to keep their affairs private and out of the local archdeacon's or bishop's court.

Between 1655 and 1660, all wills were automatically proved by the PCC, regardless of geography or status. To make matters even more complicated, certain parts of the country were under the jurisdiction of individuals or bodies other than the archdeacon or the bishop. These districts are known as 'Peculiars', and were taken care of by parish clergy, for example, or the Lord of the Manor, or else some other appointed person. To establish which places are indeed Peculiars one should consult a parish map of the county concerned, either at the County Record Office or by approaching the local family-history society.

Indexes of PCC wills are readily available in Record Offices and libraries, and local-history collections may have printed editions. Wills thus proved for the years 1383–1858 and recorded in indexes and calendars (lists with summaries of the wills' contents) are to be found at the Public Record Office, Chancery Lane, and those proved by the Prerogative Court of York from 1389 until 1858 are kept at the Borthwick Institute of Historical Research (St Anthony Hall, York).

Wills proved by local ecclesiastical courts, namely those of an archdeacon or bishop, should be lodged in the appropriate Diocesan Office, which is usually the County Record Office. The Record Offices may have microfilm copies of wills not actually held by them but relevant to their area. Thus many wills which have been destroyed since they were catalogued or filmed may be recorded in greater or lesser detail. A notable example of the dangers of keeping all one's eggs in one basket was supplied by Devon County Record Office which was unlucky enough to lose many priceless documents as a result of enemy action during World War II.

For Welsh wills proved before 1858, one should consult the National Library of Wales at Aberystwyth, and for Scottish testaments from 1514 to 1823 the Old Register House in Edinburgh. Later Scottish testaments, apart from those for Edinburgh itself (which continue to be sent to the old Register House), are held by the local Sheriff Court.

Irish wills, like so many other documents, were tragically depleted by fire during the Troubles of 1922. Those which survive, and any abstracts made, are to be found in the Irish Public Record Offices in Dublin and Belfast.

10
Afterword

And so we come to the end of our journey through the life of our imaginary ancestor. We have followed his or her progress from the cradle to the grave, and seen how he or she was buried and how his or her estate was administered. This would seem, then, the end of the line, but, of course, nothing to do with human beings is ever that straightforward.

Much of the fascination, and indeed the frustration, of family-history research lies in the fact that we never know what lies ahead; will it be weeks, months or years even, of donkey-work with little or no results, or will we stumble upon that chance clue which will set us off again on a new and exciting track? What about the newly discovered branch of the family, or the in-laws who provide another line of descent to work on? With such research you need never give up; nor need you do more than you feel like attempting at any one time. There may be a certain satisfaction to be obtained from a job which is successfully completed and put away, but what real value has a finished game of Scrabble, or a completed crossword?

Nor will our findings concerning our ancestors' lives come to light in a neat and orderly fashion. The first mention which we come across concerning great-great-great-grandfather will probably be when great-great-grandfather was christened, but what about all the years before that? Will we find his burial first, or his marriage, or perhaps his own baptism? Facts have to be collected before they can be marshalled into strict sequences, and you may have one of your ancestors jotted down in your notes for years before you can begin to claim him or her as the genuine article.

The motto, therefore, is never give up; if you become weary, change course, or give yourself a break and put the whole scruffy heap into a drawer until next winter's long, dark evenings make you look around for something to do in the warm by the fireside.

Family tree of Holmes of Devon
(Courtesy of Robin Holmes of Oxfordshire Family History Society)

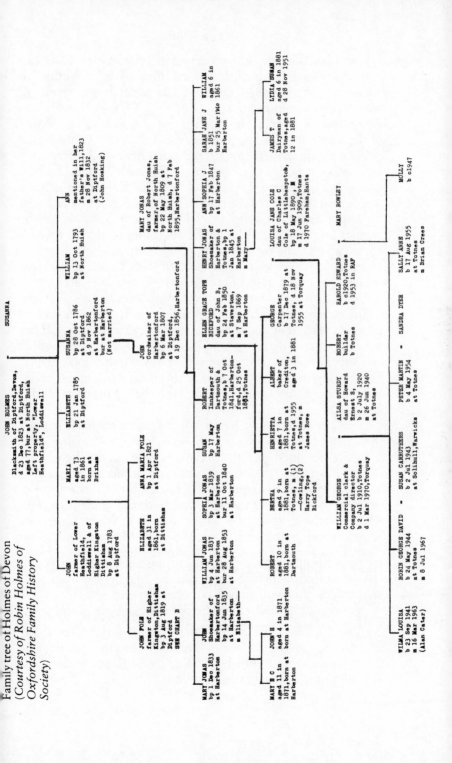

Finally, while on the subject of the imaginary ancestor, consider this example of the creation of a collection of ancestors, one which, I imagine, has never been attempted before or since. In February 1684, King Charles II, who was very proud of his Stuart blood, decided to have all his ancestors of the Scottish royal line painted. He therefore commissioned one James de Witt to undertake portraits of all 110 of his forebears 'in large royall posture'. The unfortunate de Witt signed a contract to the effect that he undertook to deliver, within two years of the contract being signed, and at a salary of £120 per annum, all these royal gentlemen (and one gentlewoman) to Holyrood House. Furthermore he had to provide his own paint and canvas, so that he was turning out Scottish monarchs at the rate of just over one a week for the sum of just over £2 per portrait, less than the cost of the materials.

Not only did de Witt have to comply with the terms of the contract, a mammoth undertaking in itself; he also had to produce a different kingly face for each picture. As many, if not the majority, of them were mythical anyway, neither de Witt nor anyone else had the slightest idea of what they looked like. The more recent ones would have been easy enough, Charles himself, with his father and grandfather, but what about Duncan, Macbeth or Corbredus I?

De Witt noticed that Charles II had a rather prominent nose; in fact, not to put too fine a point on it, he had a long and large nose. So, reasoned de Witt, to create a true family likeness, he should paint all 110 monarchs with similar noses. This seems to have been quite acceptable to Charles, but is certainly very startling to the modern viewer who finds the tendency somewhat overdone, especially when applied to Mary Queen of Scots, the only woman in the collection. Mary has not gone down in history for the size of her nose, whatever else she was famous or infamous for, so the sight of her with one which is a little reminiscent of a carrot stuck into a snowman is somewhat disconcerting.

The ironic thing about the whole business is that, although de Witt completed his part of the bargain and delivered the whole series by 1686, Charles himself died in the February of the previous year, and therefore had a first-hand opportunity of finding out just what his ancestors did look like without seeing the results of de Witt's labours!

Some Useful Addresses

England and Wales

(AGRA) Association of Genealogists and Record Agents, Mrs Jean Tooke, 1 Woodside Close, Caterham, Surrey CR3 6AU. Provides a list of members and their specialities.

British Library, Reader Admissions, Department of Printed Books, Great Russell Street, London WC1B 3DG, tel (01)-636 1544. The Library is due to move to new premises near King's Cross in the early 1990s.

County Record Offices: See J. S. W. Gibson's *Record Offices: How to Find Them*, or look in the appropriate telephone directory under the local authority.

Federation of Family History Societies (FFHS), c/o Birmingham and Midland Institute, Margaret Street, Birmingham B3 3BS.

Federation of Family History Societies (FFHS), Mrs Nora Porter, 17 Foxlea Road, Hayley Green, Halesowen, West Midlands B63 1DX.

Manorial Society of Great Britain, 65 Belmont Hill, London SE13 5AX, tel (01)-852 0200. Has an index of manors, and their lords and stewards.

National Library of Wales, Aberystwyth, Dyfed SY23 3BU, tel 0970 3816/3817. Admission by ticket; apply in writing in advance. Open Mon–Fri 9.30am to 6pm, Sat 9.30am to 5pm. Holds diocesan records for all Wales, over 400 parish registers, and pre-1858 Welsh wills.

Parish churches: See in *Crockford's Clerical Directory* under the place, or in the appropriate diocesan yearbook. Incumbents are entitled to charge a fee.

Principal Probate Registry, Somerset House, Strand, London WC2, tel (01)-405 7641. Open Mon–Fri 10am to 4.30pm. No charge to search indexes; small reading and copying fee.

Public Record Office, Chancery Lane, London WC2A 1LR, tel (01)-405 0741. Reader's ticket needed. Open Mon–Fri 9.30am to 5pm. Closed for stocktaking for first two full weeks in October.

Public Record Office, Ruskin Avenue, Kew, Richmond, Surrey TW9 4DU, tel (01)-876 3444. Details as above.

Public Record Office, Land Registry Building, Portugal Street, London WC2A 1LR, tel (01)-405 3488.

Royal Commission on Historical Manuscripts, Quality House, Quality Court, Chancery Lane, London WC2A 1HP, tel (01)-242 1198.

Record Office of the House of Lords, London SW1A 0PW, tel (01)-219 3074/3000. Search Room open Mon–Fri 9.30am to 5pm. Closed for stocktaking last two weeks of November. Written application stating nature of research requested at least one week in advance.

St Catherine's House, 10 Kingsway, London WC2B 6JP, tel (01)-242 0262. Open Mon–Fri 8.30am to 4.30pm. Entrance and access to indexes free; charge for copies of certificates.

Society of Genealogists Library, 14 Charterhouse Buildings, London EC1M 7BA, tel (01)-251 8790/8799.

Scotland

General Register Office for Scotland, New Register House, Edinburgh EH1 3YT, tel (031)-556 3952. Open Mon–Thurs 9.30am to 4.30pm, Fri 9.30am to 4.00pm. Pamphlets available giving fees for searches and certificates, and a list of accredited searchers.

Scots Ancestry Research Society, 20 York Place, Edinburgh EH1 3EP. A trust set up in 1945 by the Secretary of State for Scotland to help those with Scots ancestry.

Scottish Association of Genealogists and Record Agents, 106 Brucefield Avenue, Dunfermline. Provides a list of Scottish researchers, available from the Secretary.

Scottish Record Office, HM General Register House, Edinburgh EH1 3YY, tel (031)-556 6585/557 1022. Open Mon–Fri 9am to 4.45pm. No fees charged. Series of leaflets available on request.

Note: There are no County Record Offices in Scotland as there are in England and Wales, and so all research must take place either in the parish, in the case of registers still held by the incumbent, or in Edinburgh. The exceptions are Scottish wills from outside

Edinburgh which are held by the local Sheriff Court if proved after 1824.

Northern Ireland, the Irish Republic and the Isle of Man

Genealogical Office, Kildare Street, Dublin 2, tel Dublin 765521.

General Registry of the Isle of Man, Finch Road, Douglas, Isle of Man, tel 0624 75212. Open Mon– Fri 9am to 4.30pm. Holds pre-1878 Manx parish registers, and birth, marriage and death indexes for this year onwards. Copies of certificates issued for a fee.

Irish Family History Society, William Street, Tullamore, Co Offaly Ireland.

Irish Genealogical Association, 164 Kingsway, Dunmurray, Belfast BT17 9AD. Concentrates on research for people overseas of Northern Irish descent.

National Library of Ireland, Kildare Street, Dublin 2. Holds microfilms of some parish registers. Admission by ticket only.

Public Record Office of Ireland (now The National Archives), Four Courts, Dublin 7, tel Dublin 725275. In Irish: An Oifig Taifead Poiblí, Na Ceithre Cúirteanna, Baile Átha Cliath 7.

Public Record Office of Northern Ireland, 66 Balmoral Avenue, Belfast BT9 6NY, tel 0232 661621. Appointment necessary. Produces a series of separate guides to each county. Open Mon–Fri 9.30am to 4.30pm. Searches undertaken for a fee by the Ulster Historical Foundation, c/o PRO.

Registrar General for Ireland, Joyce House, 8–11 Lombard Street East, Dublin 2, tel Dublin 711000. In Irish: Oifig an Ard-Chlaraitheora. Open Mon–Fri 9.30am to 5pm.

Registrar General for Northern Ireland, Oxford House, 49–55 Chichester Street, Belfast 1, tel Belfast 235211. Open Mon–Fri 9.30am to 3.30pm.

State Paper Office, Birmingham Tower, The Castle, Dublin 2, tel Dublin 792777. Houses those records which, before Partition, belonged to the Chief Secretary's Office; particularly good for records concerning convictions and sentences, including transportation.

Ulster Historical Foundation, 68 Balmoral Avenue, Belfast BT9 6NY.

Note: Unfortunately, there would appear to be a shortage of professional researchers in the Irish Republic. The best advice is to ask the PRO at Dublin for recommendations, and then be prepared to wait! As already stated on page 13, there are no County Record Offices in Ireland as there are in England and Wales, and so all research must take place either in the parish, in the case of registers still held by the incumbent, or in Dublin or Belfast.

Australia

Archives Office of New South Wales, 2 Globe Street, The Rocks, Sydney, NSW 2000, tel (02) 237 0152.

Australian Archives, PO Box 34, Dickson, ACT 2602, tel 062 433633. Issue a wide variety of guides.

Australian Institute of Genealogical Studies, PO Box 68, Oakleigh, Victoria 3166.

Australian National University Library, Canberra, ACT 2602.

National Library of Australia, Parkes Place, Canberra, ACT 2600, tel (062) 61 1111.

Society of Australian Genealogists, Richmond Villa, 120 Kent Street, Observatory Hill, Sydney, NSW 2000.

State Library of New South Wales, Macquarrie Street, Sydney, NSW 2000. Includes the important Mitchell Library.

State Library of Tasmania, 91 Murray Street, Hobart, Tas 7000, tel (002)-30-8033.

New Zealand

National Archives of New Zealand, PO Box 6162, Te Aro, Wellington.

New Zealand Federation of Family History Societies, PO Box 13301, Armagh, Christchurch.

New Zealand Society of Genealogists, PO Box 8795, Auckland 3.

Registrar General of Births, Deaths and Marriages, Private Bag, Lower Hutt, Wellington.

Note: Obviously not strictly New Zealand addresses, the Archives Office of New South Wales, and the State Libraries of New South Wales and of Tasmania may be of use to New Zealand family historians, as much material relative to that country in its early days may be found in New South Wales in particular, owing to the fact that New Zealand was at first governed from Sydney, and that early immigrants often arrived there before going on to New Zealand. See Australian addresses.

SOME USEFUL ADDRESSES

The United States

Genealogical, family-history and local-history societies abound all over the United States at state, county and city level, and so it is not possible to list them all here. If you live in the USA it is best to approach your local society, which, if necessary, will be able to put you in touch with any others of interest to you, including British ones. Some useful addresses for both do-it-yourselfers and those who need some professional help are as follows:

Board for Certification of Genealogists, 1307 New Hampshire Avenue NW, Washington DC, 20036. Puts enquirers in touch with accredited genealogists who will help trace emigrant ancestors for a fee.

Family History Library of the Mormon Church, 50 East North Temple, Salt Lake City, Utah, 84150. Open Mon 7.30am to 6pm, Tues–Fri 7.30am to 10am, Sat 7.30am to 5pm. *No* research services. Issues lists of holdings, addresses of other Mormon libraries in the USA and worldwide; produces copies of the IGI microfiches for a nominal amount.

National Archives and Records Service, General Services Administration, Washington DC, 20408. Good for passenger arrivals, records of military service, pensions, etc. Recommended booklet, *Guide to Genealogical Records in the National Archives.*

The Genealogical Helper, issued by Everton Publishers Inc, PO Box 368, Logan, Utah 84321.

Canada

Public Archives of Canada, 395 Wellington Street, Ottawa, K1A 0N3. Free booklet available, *Tracing your Ancestors in Canada.*

Alberta Genealogical Society, Box 12015, Edmonton, Alberta T5J 3L2.

British Columbia Genealogical Society, Box 94371, Richmond, British Columbia V6Y 2A8.

Manitoba Genealogical Society, 420–167 Lombard Avenue, Winnipeg, Manitoba R3B 0T6.

New Brunswick Genealogical Society, PO Box 3235, Station B, Fredericton, New Brunswick E3A 2W0.

Nova Scotia Historical Society, Genealogical Committee, 57 Primrose Street, Dartmouth, Nova Scotia B3A 4C6.

Ontario Genealogical Society, Suite 253, 40 Orchard View Boulevard, Toronto, Ontario, M4R 1B9.

Prince Edward Island Genealogical Society, Box 2744, Charlotte-town, Prince Edward Island C1A 8C4.

Quebec Family History Society, PO Box 1026, Pointe Claire, Quebec H9S 4H9.

Saskatchewan Genealogical Society, 1870 Lorne Street, Regina, Saskatchewan S4P 2L7.

South Africa

Human Sciences Research Council, Private Bag X41, Pretoria 0001.

South African Genealogical Society, 40 Haylitt Street, Strand 7140. Undertakes research for a fee.

Genealogical Society of South Africa, PO Box 3057, Coetzenburg 7602.

Addresses of Embassies and High Commissions in London:

Australian High Commission, Australia House, Strand, London WC2, tel (01)-438 8000.

Canadian High Commission (Press and Information Section), Canada House, Trafalgar Square, London SW1, tel (01)-629 9492.

New Zealand High Commission, New Zealand House, Haymarket, London SW1, tel (01)-930 8422.

South African Embassy, South Africa House, Trafalgar Square, London WC2, tel (01)-930 4488.

United States Embassy, 24 Grosvenor Square, London W1, tel (01)-499 9000.

Note: Embassies, High Commissions and other national representatives in the United Kingdom and the Republic of Ireland have specialist libraries concerning their respective nations, which may be of help to family historians, particularly in the fields of immigration and emigration, geography, history and economics. Addresses and telephone numbers may be found in the appropriate Yellow or Golden Pages.

Glossary

Advowson   The right of presentation to a vacant benefice.

Affidavit   Signed certificate to the effect that a body was buried in wool.

Agricola   Tenant farmer, or any worker on the land.

Anglican Communion (churches of the)   The Church of England, the Church of Ireland, the Church of Scotland and the Church in Wales.

Archdeacon   Anglican clergyman ranking immediately below a bishop and having duties under him, such as the holding of an Archdeacon's Court.

Armiger   Person entitled to bear heraldic arms, or a squire carrying the armour of a knight in the Middle Ages.

BMD   Births, marriages and deaths. The 'B' can also stand for 'Baptisms' although it is less confusing to use the letter 'C' (for christenings).

Bann Book   Special book kept with the parish records in which marriages of parishioners outside their home parish were recorded.

Bill of Mortality   List of all those who had died in the parish, drawn up by the Parish Clerk and mentioning some fascinating causes of death. The most famous examples are those issued during the Plague of 1665.

Brasses   Engraved pieces of brass set into a church wall or floor to commemorate the deceased. English brasses, which continued until modern times, are among the finest in the world, and usually, but not always, show a picture of the dead person, and so are valuable illustrations of costume and armour.

CMB   Christenings, marriages and burials.

C of E   The Church of England.

CRO   County Record Office.

Calendar   List of documents with summaries of their contents.

Candlemas   2 February, a Scottish Quarter Day (*qv*)

Chrisom   Child who has died around the time of its baptism, so called from the white christening robe which then became its shroud.

Churchwarden   Parish office of great antiquity. Duties included the care of parish property and cash, helping with the register, etc. At least two wardens were appointed and sometimes as many as four.

Civil registration The compulsory recording of births, marriages and deaths, and the issuing of certificates for the same. Dates at which this became compulsory vary from country to country.

Constable Another ancient parish office, this time dealing with wrong-doers, inspecting alehouses, the welfare of the poor, apprenticing pauper children and helping with the training of the local militia. Not surprisingly this was not a popular position, and it was not uncommon to find deputies being paid to do the job.

County boundary changes On 1 April 1974 the British counties were reorganised. Some lost land, some gained it, and some disappeared altogether by being merged with their larger neighbours. Some 'new' counties were created while the Welsh ones were regrouped and given Welsh names.

Court Hand Form of handwriting used in British law courts.

Crockford's Directory Directory which lists living Anglican clergy (full name _Crockford's Clerical Directory_).

DRO Diocesan Record Office (normally the same place as the County Record Office).

Dog Latin False or incorrect Latin.

Ecclesiastical Provinces Those of Canterbury, York and Armagh.

Elopement The act of running away from his master by an apprentice.

FFHS The Federation of Family History Societies.

Fillius (or filia) Populi Illegitimate child (Latin, 'child of the people').

Folio Leaf of a book or manuscript (abbreviation 'f').

Gregorian Calendar That devised by Pope Gregory XIII in 1582 in order to update the Julian Calendar. The Gregorian Calendar was not adopted in this country until 1752. (_See_ Old Style and New Style.)

Holograph Will Will written in the testator's own handwriting as opposed to being dictated to a clerk.

Incumbent The holder of a benefice – a blanket term for a vicar, rector, curate, etc.

Indenture Deed or agreement drawn up between two or more parties in duplicate with each copy having indented edges. Usually used today for a lease, or normally in the plural, of a contract between apprentice and master.

Kelly's Directories Those published until recent years for towns and cities all over the country. They list residents street by street as well as by profession.

Lady Day 25 March, one of the English Quarter Days (_qv_) and before 1752 the start of the new year. Like Michaelmas, it was a day when rents fell due.

MS (S) Manuscript(s)

Membrane Skin or parchment used either singly or stitched to

GLOSSARY

others to form a roll.

Messuage Dwelling house together with its outbuildings and the enclosed land adjacent to it.

Michaelmas 29 September, another English Quarter Day and one when rents fell due.

New Style The date as reckoned by the Gregorian Calendar introduced in Britain in 1752, in which year 3 September became 14 September in order to bring us in line with the rest of Europe.

Overseer Parish officer responsible for a particular aspect of parish life. The Overseers' Accounts often make very interesting reading.

PCA Prerogative Court of Armagh.

PCC Prerogative Court of Canterbury.

PCY Prerogative Court of York.

PRO Public Record Office.

Poll Book List of those who voted at parliamentary elections at county level (and how they voted).

Quarter Sessions Assizes held four times a year at Epiphany, Easter, Michaelmas and Midsummer.

Quit Rent Payment made by a tenant to his lord in order to be excused his customary services on the manor. Sometimes used in place of the term 'Relief' in reference to the rent due from an outgoing tenant, in order to avoid confusion with Poor Relief.

Regnal Year The day, date and month as calculated by normal reckoning is sometimes replaced by the year of the sovereign's reign. These regnal years start with his or her accession and end with his or her death.

Relief Rolls Lists of outgoing and incoming tenants of land and property of a manor, not to be confused with lists of those receiving handouts.

Relict The survivor of a married couple, usually the widow.

Sheriff Court In Scotland, court in which the judge was empowered to try all but the most serious of crimes, as well as most civil cases.

Spurious Illegitimate.

Strays Individuals appearing in parish and civil records of a county other than the one in which they resided.

TS(S) Typescripts or transcripts.

Terrier Survey or register of land.

Testament In Scotland, a general term for a will.

Testator The maker of a will and/or testament.

Vid Abbreviation for either *viduus* (widower) or *vidua* (widow).

Z Sometimes used as a substitute for the 'B' for burials in the abbreviations for 'baptisms, marriages and burials', in the same way that 'C' is used for christenings. The letter 'Z' is pronounced 'Zed' (not 'Zee') in Britain. The finality of both 'Z' and burial is obvious!

187

Bibliography

Chapter 1: Introduction

Cox, Jane and Padfield, Timothy, *Tracing Your Ancestors in the Public Record Office*, PRO Handbook No 19 (HMSO, 1984).

Family Tree Magazine, 141 Great Whyte, Ramsey, Huntingdon, Cambridgeshire PE17 1HP.

Fraser, Antonia, *The Weaker Vessel* (Methuen, 1985).

Gibson, J. S. W. and Peskett, P., *Record Offices: How to Find Them* (3rd edn).

Gibson, J. S. W. and Walcott, Michael, *Where to find the IGI* (Federation of Family History Publications, 1983)

History Today Magazine.

Hoskins, W. G., *Local History in England* (Longman, 3rd edn, 1984).

Irish Public Record Office, *A Short Guide to the Public Record Office*; also a leaflet on genealogy.

Markwell, F. C. and Saul, P., *Family Historian's Enquire Within* (Federation of Family History Societies).

McCrum, Robert, Cran, William & MacNeil, Robert, *The Story of English* (BBC Publications with Faber and Faber, 1986).

McLaughlin, E., *St Catherine's House* (FFHS).

Richardson, J., *The Local Historian's Encyclopedia* (1986 edition, Historical Publications).

Rogers, C., *The Family Tree Detective* (Manchester University Press, 1986).

Smith, Alan, *The Emergence of a Nation State 1529–1660* (Longman, 1984).

The Society of Genealogists' magazine.

Steel, D., *Discovering Your Family History*, with BBC Television, for the Series 'Family History' (1979).

Steel, D. and Taylor, L., *Family History in Focus*, (Lutterworth Press, 1984).

Stone, L. *The Family, Sex and Marriage in England 1500 to 1800* (Penguin, 1979).

Wrightson, K., *English Society 1580 to 1680.* (Hutchinson, 1982)

Chapters 2 and 3: The Overseas Branches

Arnold, R., *The Furthest Promised Land: English Villagers, New Zealand Immigrants of the 1870s* (Victoria University Press, 1981).

Hall, Nick Vine, *Tracing Your Family History in Australia* (Rigby, 1985).

Surman, P., *Oak and Maple* (Carlton Press, 1982)

Chapter 4: Parish Registers

Buck, W. S. B., *Examples of Handwriting 1550–1650* (Society of Genealogists, 1965).

Gibson, J. S. W. *Bishops' Transcripts and Marriage Licences: Their Location and Indexes* (FFHS, 2nd edn, 1985).

Grieve, H. E. P., *Examples of English Handwriting 1150–1750* (Essex Education Committee, Essex Record Office Publications, 1954).

McLaughlin, E., *Parish Registers* (FFHS, 1986).

National Index of Parish Registers, ed D. J. Steel Vols I–XIII.

Phillimore Atlas and Index of Parish Registers, ed C. R. Humphery-Smith (Phillimore, 1984).

Tate, W. E., *The Parish Chest* (Cambridge University Press, 1969).

Chapter 5: Birth and Baptism

Fraser, A., *The Weaker Vessel,* (Methuen, 1985).

McLaughlin, E., *Illegitimacy* (FFHS, 3rd edn, 1985).

Stone, L., *The Family, Sex and Marriage in England 1500 to 1800* (Penguin, 1979).

Chapter 6: Marriage

Fraser, A., *The Weaker Vessel* (Methuen, 1985).

Gibson, J. S. W., *Marriage, Census, and Other Indexes for Family Historians* (FFHS, 1985).

Gibson, J. S. W., *Bishops' Transcripts and Marriage Licences: Their Location and Indexes* (FFHS, 2nd edn, 1985).

Stone, L., *The Family, Sex and Marriage in England 1500 to 1800* (Penguin, 1979).

Chapter 7: Work and Play

Gibson, J. S. W. and West, J. *Local Newspapers Before 1920 in England, Wales and the Isle of Man: A Select List* (FFHS, 1987).

Gibson, J. S. W., *Census Returns 1841–81 on Microfilm: A Directory of Local Holdings* (FFHS, 4th edn, 1986).

Gibson, J. S. W., *The Hearth Tax, Other Late Stuart Tax Lists and the Association Oath Rolls* (FFHS, 1986).

Gibson, J. S. W., *Quarter Session Records for Family Historians* (FFHS, 1985).

Hamilton-Edwards, G. K. S., *In Search of Army Ancestry* (Phillimore, 1977).

McLaughlin, E., *The Census 1841–81* (FFHS, 1985).

Steel, D. J. and Taylor, L. *Family History in Focus* (Lutterworth Press, 1984).

Chapter 8: Parish Life

Gibson, J. S. W., *The Hearth Tax, Other Late Stuart Tax Lists and the Association Oath Rolls* (FFHS, 1986).

Gooder, E., *Latin for Local History* (Longman 2nd edn, 1978).

McLaughlin, E., *Annals of the Poor* (FFHS, 1986).

McLaughlin, E., *Simple Latin for Family Historians* (FFHS, 1987).

Tate, W. E., *The Parish Chest* (Cambridge University Press, 1969).

Williams, J. Anthony, 'Sources for Recusant History (1559–1791) in England Official Archives', Catholic Record Society Journal *Recusant History*, Vol 16, No 4 (Oct 1983).

Chapter 9: Death and Burial

Gibson, J. S. W., *Wills and Where to Find Them* (Phillimore, 1974).

Gibson, J. S. W., *A Simplified Guide to Probate Jurisdictions: Where to Look for Wills* (FFHS, 1985).

McLaughlin, E., *Somerset House Wills* (FFHS, 1985).

McLaughlin, E., *Wills before 1858* (FFHS, 1985).

Note The 'Gibson Guides' and the 'McLaughlin Guides' appear in quick succession and an eye should be kept open for new additions to the series. Both series may be obtained from the Birmingham and Midland Institute, Margaret Street, Birmingham B3 3BS.

Index